MEMORIES
OF THE
'FEW'

MEMORIES OF THE 'FEW'

A Battle of Britain Tribute
to the Men & Women of
RAF Fighter Command
1940

RICHARD C. SMITH

Mitor Publications

Published & typeset by
Mitor Publications
20 Theydon Gardens, Rainham,
Essex RM13 7TU

Copyright © Richard C. Smith 2010

ISBN 978-0-9557180-1-4

Smith, Richard C.
Memories of the 'Few'
A Battle of Britain tribute to the Men & Women
of RAF Fighter Command 1940

Printed and bound in Great Britain by
Cromwell Press Group, Trowbridge, Wiltshire

CONTENTS

Acknowledgements

Without the help and contributions from the people listed below, with personal memories, photographs and memorabilia, this book would not have been possible. I would like to thank them all for their time and knowledge, for without it this book would be far less richer. Sadly as time moves forever on, some of the contributors have passed on.

Wing Commander Peter Ayerst, DFC RAF Retd
The late Warrant Officer Fred Barker, DFM
Wing Commander Robert Barton, OBE, DFC
The late Wing Commander Eric Barwell, DFC
The late Squadron Leader George Bennions, DFC
The late Air Commodore Ronald Berry, CBE, OBE, DSO, DFC
The late Air-Vice Marshal Harold Bird-Wilson, CBE, AFC, DSO, DFC
The late Air Commodore Peter Brothers, DSO, DFC
Squadron Leader Peter Brown, AFC
The late Flight Lieutenant John Burgess
Flight Lieutenant Jimmy Corbin
Flight Lieutenant Leonard Davies
The late Squadron Leader Peter Dawburn
The late Air Commodore Alan Deere, OBE, DSO, DFC
The late Squadron Leader Desmond Fopp, AFC
Wing Commander Robert Foster, DFC
The late Squadron Leader Derek Glaser, DFC
The late Group Captain Colin Gray, DSO, DFC
Flight Lieutenant William Green, RAF Retd
The late Warrant Officer Reginald Gretton
The late Flight Lieutenant Leslie Harvey
The late Squadron Leader Carlton Haw, DFC, DFM
The late Squadron Leader Norman Hayes, DFC
The late Wing Commander William Higginson, DFC, DFM

The late Squadron Leader Iain Hutchison, TD
Flight Lieutenant Richard Jones
The Late Wing Commander John Kilmartin DFC
The late Group Captain Brian Kingcome, DSO, DFC
The late Air Commodore Donald MacDonell, CB, DFC
The late Squadron Leader Percy Morfill, DFM
Wing Commander Roger Morewood RAF Retd
Wing Commander Tom Neil, DFC, AFC
The late Group Captain Herbert Pinfold
Flight Lieutenant Denis Robinson
The late Squadron Leader Gerald Stapleton, DFC
The late Wing Commander George Unwin, DSO, DFM
The late Group Captain Edward Wells, DSO, DFC
Mrs Jessica Berryman
Mrs Joy Caldwell
Mr Nigel Carver
Mr Frank Clarke
The late Ernie Clayton
Mrs Iris Cockle
Mr Joe Crawshaw
Mr Jim Croft
The late Arthur 'Dave' Davis
Mr Glen Duhig
Mr Michael Evans
Mrs Hazel Gregory
Mr John Gill
The late Mrs Avis Hearn MM
Mr Michael Hodges
Mr John Milne
Mr Arthur Moreton
Mr David Ross
Mr Andy Saunders
Mr Jack Shenfield

Special thanks to Wing Commander Robert Foster DFC, it is an honour to have him contribute the Foreword to this book. Mr Ian Taylor, photographer and designer of the excellent book cover. Nigel Carver and Simone Knol for the front cover re-enactment, the Chesham Museum & Gwyneth Bradley for permission to use the Avis Hearn photograph

The Imperial War Museum Photographic & Sound Archive, London for all their help and assistance in photographs from their collection. The Staff at the National Archive at Kew, London. Mr Arthur Moreton for invaluable help with photographs and information regarding North Weald. Thanks once again to Colin and Rose Smith of Vector Fine Art for the book launch. To Peter Holloway and all at Cromwell Press for production and printing. The North Weald Airfield Museum and the Purfleet Heritage & Military Centre, Military Trader.co.uk. Apologies to anyone who has mistakenly been left out. Thanks go out to all the people who have bought my previous books or supported me in my efforts over the last 15 years. Finally love to my wife Kim and son's David and especially Robert who helped with the final editing.

Richard C. Smith
March 2010

FOREWORD
by
Wing Commander Robert Foster DFC
Chairman of the Battle of Britain Fighter Association

In June 1940, Winston Churchill addressing the House of Commons said, speaking of the surrender of all French Forces, 'The Battle of France is over, and I suspect the Battle of Britain will soon begin.' He was right. A few weeks later, the German Luftwaffe launched their mass attacks over Southern England with the object of destroying the Royal Air Force as a prelude to a possible invasion.

Many books have been written about the events of that Summer, detailing and analysing the strategic and tactical decisions taken by both sides, the successes and mistakes, the political in-fighting between the commanders, and of course the deeds of the airmen defending their country and defying the enemy to overcome them.

This book however, not only recounts the stories of some of these airmen, but also pays tribute to the men and women and the organisation 'behind the front line,' who together made victory possible.

The instructors at the Operational Training Units, experienced fighter pilots, but needed to train the incoming bunch of 'rookies.' The ground crews, working through the night to repair and service damaged aircraft for action the next day. The WAAFs, young girls, many from sheltered backgrounds, serving on fighter stations and radar units, who suddenly found themselves target for enemy bombings. No fewer than five were awarded the Military Medal for bravery under fire. Last but not least, the ordinary people of Britain who carried on working in offices and factories, often under arduous conditions, to help the war effort and ensure eventual victory.

As Winston Churchill truly said, 'This was their finest hour.'

Wing Commander Robert Foster DFC
March 2010

v

INTRODUCTION

It is now over 70 years since the world was thrown into the mass conflict that was the Second World War and although the years have passed and certain campaigns and battles fought fade from people's memories and history, one such battle that was fought during the summer months of 1940, seems to have remained embedded within the British nations psyche, the 'Battle of Britain.'

For 30 years after the event, very little attention was paid to this campaign of the air, although the 15th September was annually recognised as Battle of Britain Day by the Royal Air Force and small displays were organised by special open days at RAF aerodromes. It was not until the late 1980s and the birth of the Air Shows, that the general public started to learn more of the greatest air battle in history and meet some of the veterans that battled in the skies over Britain in 1940.

In the last few years, belated monuments to the 'Few' have at last been erected to pay fitting tribute to those gallant airmen from all corners of the world, who came and fought and died to keep Britain free from Nazi occupation in 1940. The two outstanding monuments that now honour the pilots and aircrew are sited at Capel-le-Ferne near Folkestone and on the Westminster Embankment in London. Both paid for by public donations.

This book I hope will help in some way to educate future generations by reading the first hand accounts of those men and women who served in RAF Fighter Command during those vital three months of this nation's history. There have been so many books written over the last 50 years covering the facts and figures, the aircraft, the commanders and their tactics.

This book covers for the first time using the veterans own stories, of how they undertook their pre-war training, the Operational Training Units, the accounts by the unsung heroes, the ground crews who worked day and night to keep the aircraft serviceable and Women's Auxiliary Air Force, who manned the operations rooms or worked the new Radar systems to give advance warning of the incoming enemy formations. The early war engagements when France and Belgium were invaded are also covered.

How did it feel to be shot down? This is also covered with the first hand accounts on tactics learnt and used by the lucky ones who survived their first few combats. The loss of comrades? How did the pilots keep morale high, while their friends around them were being killed on a daily basis and have the strength to carry on?

For the last 15-years it has been an honoured privilege to have been so lucky to be invited to visit the veterans at their homes all over this country and record their wartime memories on film for posterity. In doing so, this book is probably the last record of those heroes of the skies, as so many of them I interviewed have now passed on.

If reading this book, you have been enlightened and wish to learn more about the Battle of Britain and of those who paid the ultimate sacrifice for your freedom so many years ago, then it has been a worthwhile journey. Always remember the 'Few and the Many' who made it possible.
It was their Finest Hour!

Richard C. Smith
March 2010

CHAPTER 1

Training the 'Few'

By the mid 1930s, the expansion of the Royal Air Force was well underway, now with a possible threat looming from Germany, now under the leadership of their new Chancellor, Adolf Hitler. Hitler and the Fascist Nazi Party was coursing unease in Europe with their build up of arms and machinery, having torn up any remaining rules which had been governed by the Versailles Treaty after the First World War. In Britain, many young men now seemed eager to join the RAF, with the chance of being taught to fly for free and having a career in the service, or others who joined the RAF Volunteer Reserve or Auxiliary Air Force and University Air Squadrons to fly at weekends.

The Auxiliary Air Force was an idea pushed forward by founder of the Royal Air Force Lord Hugh Trenchard, who visualised the possibility of an elite corps of civilian fliers who could be called upon in times of war, if needed. The formation of the Auxiliary Air Force was established by Order of Council on 9th October 1924 and the first four squadrons were formed the following year. The squadrons were all given a number, the first being 500, 501, 502 and 504. Other squadrons formed started at 600 up to 616. They would also carry the titles of the 'County' or 'City' they would represent, for example 504 was 'City of Nottingham.' The formation of the AAF became so successful that by the 1939, some twenty squadrons had been formed.

Most of those who volunteered into the AAF were drawn from local areas in which their AAF headquarters were established. Training was mainly at weekends or on summer weekday evenings, with a once a year fortnight summer camp training alongside the regular RAF. By the summer of 1940, the Auxiliaries would provide 14 squadrons available of RAF Fighter Commands sixty-two, ready for the confrontation that lay ahead.

Alongside the Auxiliary squadrons was the Royal Air Force Volunteer Reserve, this had been formed in July 1936 to supplement the AAF. Initially run by civilian flying

Training the 'Few'

training schools, they employed instructors who previously had completed a four year short service commission as pilots and were now members of the Reserve of Air Force Officers. Recruits from all works of life began to volunteer. To join you had to be aged between 18 and 25 years and medically fit. The part-time training would cover the role of pilot, wireless operator and observers.

On outbreak of hostilities, any civilian volunteer accepted into the RAFVR for training would have to take an oath of allegiance. He would then be sent home and would wait to be called up for training.

During this period there was also a large influx of Commonwealth entries into the service, the largest proportion coming from Canada, Australia and New Zealand, which was most gratefully accepted and would prove to be of great necessity during the war years. So what was the inspiration for these young men and women and what facilities and training could the Royal Air Force provide? Looking back in hindsight was the training geared for a possible conflict ahead and were tactics during this time ever discussed or practiced?

So what were the main instructional aircraft being used during this period? The de Havilland DH 82 Tiger Moth biplane was designed by Geoffrey de Havilland. It was a basic aircraft, made of wood construction and covered with dope fabric with few controls; it handled well and was forgiving in the air. Communication was relayed by the instructor to the novice pilot by Gosport tube earphones.

The Royal Air Force initially ordered thirty-five duel control Tiger Moth 1s in February 1932, but replaced these with fifty more MkIIs which were powered by a 130 horse-power Gipsy Major engine. The aircraft had a top speed of 109 mph flying at 1,000 feet, a range of 300 miles and could reach a service ceiling height of 13,600 feet. By late September 1939, over 500 were in service with the RAF.

Other aircraft being used for training did include the Hawker Hart, Hind and Fury biplanes which were now obsolete as front line aircraft with the introduction of the new Hawker Hurricane and later the Supermarine Spitfire.

Training the 'Few'

Another trainer was the Miles Magister, which was a tandem two-seat low wing cantilever monoplane. It was constructed of spruce and plywood and had an open cockpit. First flown in 1937 and known 'affectionately by those who flew it as the 'Maggie' She was powered by de Havilland Gipsy Major 1 inline piston engine which produced 130 horsepower, giving a top speed of 130 mph and could reach a service ceiling of 18,000 feet. Over 700 had been produced by the outbreak of war

From across the Atlantic, enter another aircraft which was to be used for more advanced training. The North American T-6 Texan or BC-1, was known in this country as the 'Harvard 1'. This monoplane was powered by a Pratt & Witney R-1340 Wasp radial piston engine that produced an output of 600 horsepower. Top speed was 208 mph at 5,000 feet, a range of 730 miles and top altitude of 24,200 feet. In 1938, the Royal Air Force ordered several hundred of this type, to be fitted out with British instruments and radios. It was the next step up for some of the trainee pilots from biplane to monoplane, before then being sent to convert to fighter aircraft.

George Bennions hailed from Burslam, Stoke on Trent and had entered into the Royal Air Force as an aircraft apprentice at Halton in January 1929, where he was trained in all aspects of aircraft maintenance and repair and full knowledge of aircraft flying capabilities. He completed the course in December 1931, passing out as a leading aircraftsman engine fitter. He was put forward to attend the RAF College at Cranwell to become a cadet and underwent his ab-initio flying training there. But his entry as a cadet was not realised. Still eager to fly, he continued his training at Sealand and then at No. 3 FTS Grantham in Lincolnshire.

I was taught to fly on Avro 504s for the elementary training and Bristol Bulldogs for service training. I took around 8 hours before I went solo. I then flew Siskin biplanes during my advanced training. In February 1936, I was then posted to No. 41

Squadron which at that time was serving out in the Middle East at Khormaksar, Aden. I was then a sergeant pilot. Here I was introduced to two-seater Demon fighters and they didn't trust me to fly with a passenger for the first few flights. Sergeant Steere, he was an excellent pilot and he took me on local flying for recognition of the local countryside which consisted of a lot of sand dunes, they all became familiar as they looked all the same to me.

On one occasion I took off to do some aerobatics with Corporal Holden as a passenger, that worried me to death because when I landed, I looked over and the rear seat was empty and I'd thought I lost him somewhere over the desert. Apparently, my aerobatics had been so awful that he had finished up in the back of the fuselage. Other training included practice dive-bombing and formation flying, the dive bombing at that time was used against any unruly tribes. The squadron was posted back to Catterick in Yorkshire in August 1936.

Back in England, we were given the Hawker Fury Mk2; it was a lovely aircraft to fly and was excellent for aerobatics. The squadron attended the Empire Air Day displays and we would be decked out in our clean white flying suits emblazoned with the squadron crest just below the left breast pocket to impress the public.

On 21st June 1938, I went to a practice camp and didn't know what to expect, but this is when I started to feel like a real fighter pilot. The following day I was sent to RAF Aldergrove in Northern Ireland to undertake air to air firing against a drogue which was being towed and we had to shoot at it the best we could. I had only fired eighty rounds, but I got a score of seventy-five on the target. What I didn't realise was that the bullet made two holes, so I was very disappointed; I had got less than half on the target. The following day I improved slightly with two hundred rounds fired, my score went up to one hundred and thirteen. My percentage of hits rose steadily over the next few days and on one occasion I shot the drogue away completely.

After 582 hours flying time, I was assessed to see how competent I was in flying, my commanding officer wrote 'completed fighter training day and night on 11th August 1938' and I was classed as 'proficient as a pilot on the type, on Demon aircraft–average and on Hawker Fury II aircraft, above the average. I was very pleased.

On 13th January 1939, I undertook my first flight in a Spitfire. I took off at 2.15 pm in the afternoon and flew for 1 hour-15 minutes and it was supposed to be to gain experience on the type, but somehow, somewhere I lost the tail-wheel and I caused a great big furrow in the earth when I landed. I tried to keep the weight off the tail by pushing the stick forward. My first night flight in a Spitfire was on 9th March 1939, and I did 1 hour - 45 minutes just local flying using the radio telephone and direction finding to get back to the aerodrome. My logbook also shows that we even did night-flying practice in flight and squadron formation, which was interesting to say the least.

Nineteen year old Roger Morewood who had attended the Edinburgh College of Art decided that he would enter into the Royal Air Force in 1935. He walked into the Air Ministry in London and asked how he could join the service and told them that he wanted to fly. He was accepted into the RAF and joined as a direct entry Airman under-training Pilot.

I was first sent to No. 4 Elementary Flying School up in Brough which is near Hull that September. I trained on a weird biplane aircraft called a B2E, which was a bit like a Tiger Moth, but had side by side seating. From there I was sent to Desford to fly Tiger Moths and once I had completed my training and gone solo, which from my logbook shows was eight hours; I was commissioned and was sent to Uxbridge for square bashing, which I already had done anyway. My next stop was Grantham at 3 FTS. There was no tactics discussed during this period, we just enjoyed flying. We practiced on Audax aircraft and because I didn't crash any of them, they gave me a Hawker Fury fighter to fly and in my logbook I got an above average assessment written in by the flight commander.

I was then sent to dear old famous No. 56 Squadron at North Weald near Epping in Essex in May 1937. When I arrived the squadron was flying Gloster Gauntlets, we then received Gladiators and then finally Hawker Hurricanes.

It was marvellous to be part of an operational squadron, especially No. 56 as we were always being reminded of the previous pilots who had served during the First World War, the likes of aces Albert Ball and James McCudden and we always had that idea of living up to their standards.

The Hawker Hurricane was a wonderful aeroplane; I would prefer that any day to a

Spitfire. I had flown many a Spitfire for fun, I flew about 20-30 hours on them, but the horribly knock kneed undercarriage was not as stable as the old Hurricanes.

While with 56 Squadron, I had just done a fraction off 200-hours on Hurricane aircraft and I had passed my exams for promotion and to get a permanent commission. I passed my exams alright, I got promoted to flight lieutenant, but the sad thing was, they said at the Air Ministry 'Sorry boy's no more permanent commissions, you can get a war service commission.' So I didn't get a pension when I left.

Thomas Norman Hayes, born in 1912, was educated at Dulwich College and then studied engineering at university; he joined the Auxiliary Air Force in July 1936

I joined 600 Squadron which was the 'City of London' Auxiliary Squadron in 1936 and I was trained to fly with them at Hendon. I was taught to fly on an Avro 504, which was a biplane from the old First World War design and on a duel control Hawker Hart. It took me about ten hours which was about average. The squadron was later re-equipped with Hawker Demons in 1938 and was called up during the Munich Crisis in August that year with these aircraft still wearing their silver livery. They were a wonderful aeroplane, open cockpit and very nice to fly. Fortunately by the time war was declared in September 39, the squadron had already been converted over to the Bristol Blenheim, which was a light bomber. I found the Blenheim quite an easy aircraft to fly, we had been given instruction on a converted duel control aircraft, although of course you noticed the increase in power and weight from biplane to twin engine monoplane. The squadron did participate in the home defence exercises during this period, but personally I thought they were a waste of time and never took them seriously. We heard that war was imminent when we were at our war station at Northolt.

Peter Brown was eighteen years of age and had been accepted into the RAF on a short service commission in 1938, he was then sent on an Ab-Initio Training Course at Hansworth in Middlesex on 4th April 1938. The course would last six weeks and the new candidates would be given sixty hours of flying training. An estimated 20% of those would fail.

Hanworth was a flying club as were all the other twenty elementary flying schools used by the RAF. It was the first time we had met our other colleagues and we were all still civilians. We were housed in a large building in the middle of the aerodrome, where we ate, slept and had our lectures. Here I was trained on an aircraft called the Blackburn B2. This was different from most trainers in that the pupil and instructor sat side by side, so that the relationship was total and not through a piece of voice pipe tubing. I went solo after about ten hours, which was about average. To go solo in eight hours was very good, but if you hadn't gone solo by twelve to thirteen hours, there would be grave doubts about proceeding any further with flying training.

I did a total of sixty hours flying there by day and carried out the standard programme of take-offs, landings, turns, climbs spinning and cross-country.

Training the 'Few'

Eric Barwell decided he would join the Royal Air Force Volunteer Reserve. His older brother Philip had joined in 1925 on a short service commission. Eric had been at school one day when his brother had dropped a message to him from his aircraft tied to a weighted streamer, for Eric this was adventurous and exciting, he could not wait until he would be old enough to learn to fly:

> I joined the RAFVR at Cambridge in July 1938, but I did have some trouble at first qualifying to get in? I was sent to undertake a medical and one of the first people to see me was the optician. He examined me and told me that I had Xophoria, a condition where the eyes splay out, the opposite to cross-eyed and that I would never be able to fly. I had always prided myself on my good eyesight, so I contacted my brother and he thought it sounded a bit strange. He invited me up to visit him at Digby, where he was stationed for the weekend. While there, he took me up in a Miles Magister and we did circuits and bumps. He would ask me to tell him just when we were about to land and each time I told him correctly. He then sent this information to the chief optician at the Central Medical Establishment and I was duly summoned up to London, where I passed all the tests and was eventually accepted. I was then sent to No. 22 Elementary Flying School at Marshall's aerodrome, Cambridge and was trained on Tiger Moths, Hawker Harts and Hind biplanes.

Peter Ayerst from Westcliffe near Southend-on Sea was just eighteen, when his first flying experience arrived by chance in 1938; it was an experience that would change his way of life forever.

9

Training the 'Few'

I had a friend, Don Wallace, a friend of our family, who had quite a lot of money and owned an aircraft and it was a two seat job, he had a private pilot's license and a B license which made it possible for him to fly commercial. He said to me 'have you ever been flying' and I said 'No', he said would you like to go and I said 'Yes'. This was in early 1938, he then took me up in his aircraft for about three quarters of an hour and flew me around and did a few turns and twists, when we landed I told him I had thoroughly enjoyed it and he replied 'you must come up again.' The following week I went up again, but it was a bit more advanced this time and it was very good. The summer was just beginning in '38 and he said I've got to go to Romford to take people for flights and if you would like to come over with me, we can set up a table, you can take the money and help strap them in and as they come down you can help them out. I can remember it was a lovely summer and we continued to do this for a couple of weeks, and this was where I got my first feeling towards flying.

Soon after I saw that the RAF were advertising for pilots for short service commissions, four years active service and six years on reserve. As I couldn't afford to learn to fly myself I thought that sounded good, I'll have a go at that. I applied and I had to go for an interview at the Air Ministry, which was then at Kingsway, London. When I arrived there they told me to go and have a medical test first, because if I didn't pass, that there was no point continuing the interview. I passed that OK and then was asked to wait, I was then put into a room where five distinguished looking chaps were seated and they asked various questions. I was there for about half an hour and answered the best I could. They thanked me for coming and said they would let me know the result of my visit here within two weeks. I must admit when I walked out I didn't feel very confident, because they seemed such a powerful and intimidating group. However I received the letter and found I had been accepted.

I started my service on 6th October 1938 and undertook my elementary training at Gatwick in Surrey; this was the first RAF flying course from there. Gatwick was just a small grass airfield, no runways. They only had one large building there at the time called the Beehive, it was here we kept our flying kit, we would change there for flying, and we also had a restaurant and a lounge to relax, but we didn't sleep there, we were billeted out. I and another chap were billeted at a house in Crawley.

At Gatwick, I was on the very first RAF course training on Miles Magisters', it was the RAF's first monoplane trainer, all the other elementary training units had Tiger Moths. Here I completed about sixty hours flying.

Following my completion at Gatwick, I was then sent to Grantham in Lincolnshire for the advanced flying, thinking we would be put on Hawker Harts or something like that, but no I was fortunate to be one of the first trainee pilots in the RAF to learn on the new Harvard. I was there for about nine months and flew about 140-hours on this type and completed my training about three months before war was declared; I was then posted to No. 73 Squadron at Digby, who had Mk 1 Hawker Hurricanes with the two-bladed airscrew.

Jimmy Corbin from Maidstone in Kent was 22 years old, when he applied to join the RAFVR.

> From a very young age I was keen on flying and I wanted to fly. I was in full time education till the age of twenty-one and the RAF had a ruling you couldn't join the Volunteer Reserve until you finished your full time education. I finished my full time education in August 1938, so I re-applied and I got in straight away.
>
> There was no war when I joined the RAF, but as we got near to 1939, when war became a distinct possibility, every able bodied man or boy joined something, the Territorial Army, the Air Force or the Navy; they joined something because we were very loyal in those days and patriotic to King and Country. The RAFVR had an office in the Chatham/Rochester area and here we had lectures for the first year and I didn't start flying until about June 39. Joining the VR you were given a uniform straight away, you had to do 15-days straight in one go in a year. I took longer to do solo, about 16 hours, it wasn't because I was a bad pilot, it was not continuous flying training and I could only fly weekends from Rochester Aerodrome. I trained and flew solo on Miles Magisters.
>
> I was mobilised a fortnight before war was declared – the RAF was so badly organised in those days, they did not know what to do with us, so they sent me to an I.T.W (Initial Training Wings). I went to a college in Cambridge University; we were stationed

there with a regular flight sergeant and drill instructor that was in charge. He wasn't a bad chap, he used to get us up in the morning and then about 10.30 am, we would go for a march out of the college and when we got to the nearest pub, which was about two miles away, we used to stop and buy the flight sergeant a lot of beer, he was happy with that and then we used to turn around and come back, that was all the square bashing we did.

The RAF training in those days, you had three sections, the initial training which was on Magisters in my case, then you did the intermediate which was a more powerful aircraft, in my case it was the Harvard, then the advanced training school. Overall this took roughly 50 hours in each section, which took quite some time. Then you were sent to operational training unit, whichever OTU you went too depended on the luck of the draw. In my case I got into fighters, I had wanted to go into Coastal Command, because I wanted to fly a Sunderland flying boat, I'd been in one but never flown one as a pilot.

Ernest 'Dave' Glaser had always wanted to fly, it was in his blood. His father had served in the Royal Flying Corps during the First World War and now ran a local public house not far from Eastleigh aerodrome, where young 'Dave' was always eager to visit. Eastleigh was where Reginald Mitchell's prototype Spitfire had first flown and test pilot Jeffrey Quill was a frequent visitor to the Bugle Pub, owned by 'Dave's father. At the age of 18, he was accepted into the Royal Air Force Volunteer Reserve for flying training at No.3 Elementary Flying School at Hamble.

Training the 'Few'

My first instructor, Flying Officer Winton
was very good and he said that he wanted to
put me on a Tiger Moth aeroplane. He
reckoned that if you could fly a Tiger you
could learn to fly anything and he was right. I
liked the Tiger immensely and I did my first
solo on 29th August 1939. The chief
instructor had taken me up and we did a few
flying procedures, then we came in and
landed. He said 'well do another take-off' so
I taxied around ready to go again. Then he
stood up and stepped out of the cockpit in
front of me and said 'off you go.' I did a
circuit and made a complete muck up of the
landing, too high and too far down, so I
went around again and made a peach of a
landing just be pure chance. When I taxied
in, I said 'I made a mess of that.' Flying
Officer Fenton, the instructor said, 'No
you're alright, you went around again no
trouble at all.

It had taken Dave Glaser 13 hours and 55 minutes to train
and go solo. A few days later on 3rd September Britain
declared war on Germany and he was ordered to travel to
Hastings in Sussex.

We gathered at Hastings, waiting to be
posted to an airfield for further training. In
November, I was sent to No.1 Elementary
Flying Training School at Hatfield, flying
Tiger Moths again. I remained here until
mid-March 1940 and after logging 41 hours
duel flying and 33 hours solo, I was then sent
to Little Rissington in Gloucester to No. 6
Flying Training School. It was here I was
introduced to the North American Harvard
training aircraft, but we did most of our
flying at Kidlington. After a few weeks spent

here, I achieved an above average rating and instead of then going to an operational training unit as most chaps did, I was sent straight away to an operational squadron. In my case to No. 65 Squadron based at Hornchurch in Essex.

Charlton 'Wag' Haw was born in Yorkshire on 8th May 1920, he remembers those early days in the RAF; he would eventually go on to become one of the RAF's most successful fighter pilots and squadron leaders of the war:

When I left school I worked for three months in an iron-mongers shop until there was a vacancy at William Sessions which was a lithographic printers and I managed to get an apprenticeship. I joined the RAF Volunteer Reserve the moment I reached eighteen, which meant you could be taught to fly at weekends. I failed the medical through eyesight in October 1938 and was given some exercises to do, I then went back in January '39 and passed the eye test and was then granted a place in the VR as a pilot under training. I had always wanted to fly since I had been a small boy; I had never wanted to do anything else really. I didn't really think I would get a chance, because most of the people had come from universities with very high educational qualifications and they went into the short service commissions of the RAF at that time and the chances of any normal school boy to get in, were until the VR was formed was almost impossible.

I went solo in a third of the time that was average for the new pilot, which was twelve hours; I did it in 4-hours 40 minutes. My instructor said I was a natural pilot. Could have been because I played the piano, the gentle touch and they say that pianists and horsemen make the best pilots; I don't know if that is true or not?

I did my training at Brough near Hull in East Yorkshire. We did three nights a week on theory and flying at the weekend. As soon as I started to fly I was given two-weeks off work to do 14-days concentrated flying and had done 80-hours by the time war was declared. I had just started to fly bigger aircraft like Harts and Hinds. When we heard war had been declared I'm afraid we all let off a big cheer. It's a terrible thing to say, but the chance to be given a Spitfire or Hurricane was a school boys dream come true and we didn't think about our own danger.

The most disappointing thing was soon after we were all sent home, visions of sitting in a Spitfire or Hurricane had been shattered. A month passed and I was then sent to an ITW (initial training wing) at Bexhill in Sussex, where we did parades which was frustrating in a way, then in December, several of us were posted to Sealand in Cheshire for intermediate and advanced training. My assessment while under training gave me above average and once I finished my training in May 1940, I then received a posting to go to an OTU, but France fell and I received a phone call telling me to report direct to No. 504 Squadron based at Wick in Scotland who were equipped with Hawker Hurricanes.

Within a month of joining that squadron I had my first combat. Being raw and too keen, I got a bullet right through the canopy, how it missed me I'll never know. It was from a Heinkel 111 over Scapa Flow at 7.00 am in the morning. Three of us had been vectored through some layers of cloud, it was murky. We came out of cloud and there was the Heinkel. Our commanding officer dived down after it, his No. 2 followed him down and I followed them in. As we got close, you could see the rear-gunner firing what looked like red hot chain links coming out of the gun, the aircraft dived into cloud, but we didn't shoot it down as we were then too far away; but as I broke away one bullet came through my cockpit. When I got back the chaps were all slapping me on the back saying how lucky I was.

Pilot Officer George Bennions:

When war broke, what really annoyed me was the Air Ministry took out all of the really good experienced pilots, I am mainly talking about the regular sergeants and flight sergeants, and they took them all out of the squadrons and put them into flying training schools, of all the stupid things to do. The impetus for me really were the sergeants and flight sergeants, they were better qualified than the rest when it came to experience they had gained.

In Fighter Command it was not only the pilots that were being trained for the forthcoming war and battle ahead, but also the women of the Women's Auxiliary Air Force, who would play an important part in manning the Operations Rooms, the important Radio Direction Finding Stations (Radar) and signals.

Avis Hearn came from the village of Chesham Bois in Buckinghamshire. Before the war, Avis had studied and worked in interior furnishings. In 1938, aged twenty-three, she joined the Buckinghamshire 39th Auxiliary Territorial Service Company at RAF Halton. In June 1939, the Women's Auxiliary Air Force was formed, so she immediately applied and became a WAAF. Avis recalls:

> I was called up straight away, had an interview and was then sent to Leighton Buzzard to learn the job of plotting at 60 Group, which was a part of radio direction finding (Radar) and was taught by Sir Robert Watson-Watt, who was the scientist who discovered Radar by accident. Once we had learnt to plot, I was sent to RAF Bentley Priory, which was the headquarters of Fighter Command. There was an enormous map table and we plotted by code receiving information from all the RDF stations situated around the coast of Britain from the tip of Cornwell to as far north as Scotland. We used what looked like giant tiddily winks and having been giving the plotting code; you would move these around the table as the information was relayed. This was filtered by the filter officer, giving out speed, height etc.
>
> I did see 'Stuffy' Dowding, the commander in chief, when he would come into the Filter Room where I worked. On the balcony above there would be other officers looking down to see what was happening, the army, navy and observer corps was all represented. 'Stuffy' would just wander in and look down on to the table. We would be told by our duty officer to sit up straight, 'the air marshal is about'
>
> The top brass then thought if the women could do this job, then perhaps we could be useful manning the RDF stations. I was then sent to Bawdsey in Suffolk in October 39.

Training the 'Few'

This was an experimental facility for radio direction finding and was set up in a big mansion like house on the coast, which the Air Ministry had requisitioned. I did about three weeks there learning how to operate this cathode ray tube machine and how to pick up an aircraft and get a bearing on it. We had to sign the official secrets act because we were being taught by a high ranking air force officer who told us that the work we would be doing was top secret and that had anybody given away information, they could be court-marshalled or even shot. It was the best kept secret of the war.

On the site were these giant transmitting aerials which were 360 feet high and receiving aerials, 280 feet in height. The transmitter would pick up the aircraft and this would appear on your screen as a little V-shaped thing, you would then read of the degrees and range, then somebody else with a slide rule would work out the information. You would have to be able to do that at four a minute. We worked on shifts, from 8.00 am till 1.00 pm, or 1.00 to 6.00 and 6.00 till midnight or midnight till 8.00 next morning; you would only get one day off.

When the war started, we were very quiet and that year we had a very bad winter, which grounded most of the aircraft over here and on the continent; but it gave us the chance to learn our equipment better.

As the weather became better, we started to get a lot busier, but it was not until France fell and the Germans could then use the French airfields that we started to pick up larger formations.

Training the 'Few'

John Milne was part of the essential ground staff that kept Fighter Command's aircraft serviceable during the Battle of Britain. Born in Folkestone in 1920, the family moving to Cambridge in 1931 and after finishing his education and war clouds looming on the horizon, John made the decision of volunteering into a service before war broke out.

It seemed by 1939 that war was certain and my father and I agreed on this, therefore I decided to volunteer in good time, presuming that the onset of war would result in chaos, panic and pressure, and by acting early I could choose my service. I decided to join the Royal Air Force towards the end of August 1939.

To join the RAF in peacetime although war was imminent, involved a lot of work. There was of course form-filling, and the provision of referees. I gave as my referees the Reverent W.W. Partridge, vicar of St. Luke's Church Cambridge, and Mr. Robinson, a solicitor's managing clerk, a family friend who lived opposite us on Milton Road.

My induction began at Adastral House, Kingsway in London, where I had arrived from Cambridge by train and tube. There was the inevitable questioning and form-filling - had I passed any RAF educational examinations? No, I had two school certificates and two higher school certificates. They gave me simple tests in English and arithmetic and were satisfied. The medical examination was tough. We stripped off and were shunted between tests until we nearly dropped. I would have been A1, but for my defective eyesight - some astigmatism and myopia, which sounds worse than it was. Anyhow, I was accepted, and had to resolve the question of what I would do in the RAF. Eventually it was agreed that I should be trained as a flight rigger - a bit of an unknown quantity. About six of us, in the charge of a uniformed sergeant, travelled by London Underground to West Drayton where, over a couple of days, we were 'sworn in' and given our RAF number. This was my introduction to the communal living and feeding of the RAF. Meal times reminded me of school dinners, but the food was better.

Then we were sent in groups by train to Padgate, a 'square-bashing' depot outside Warrington. Passing through London we saw at a main-line station the crowds of children being evacuated - not a happy sight. On 3rd September, we heard the Prime Minister Neville Chamberlain on the radio, announcing the state of war with Germany. We cheered, only to be told by our sergeant 'There's nothing to cheer about'. That, and the blue lighting in our huts, brought it home to us that things had changed. Over a period of four weeks we learned foot drill and rifle drill, which I found easy. Having been in the Officers' Training Corps (OTC) at school, I was used to the niceties of sloping arms, grounding arms, presenting arms, and changing arms on the march. We enjoyed physical training, gas drill and cross-country running, the latter sometimes in gas masks. We were issued with our uniforms and other kit, and given wrapping materials for sending home our civilian clothing. We learned the intricacies of the maintenance and the laying out of our kit for inspection, and how to polish the floor and beautify our webbing equipment.

While at Padgate I attended my first and only game of rugby league, in which Wigan beat Warrington. The cheapest beer was five pence a pint (about two new pence). Our pay was two shillings a day (ten new pence).

All good things come to an end and those of us destined to be trained as flight riggers were posted on 30th September 1939 to RAF Halton, near Wendover in Buckinghamshire. Halton was the RAF No. 1 School of Technical Training. Lord Trenchard had said that the RAF was founded on flying and engineering, and we soon found out about the engineering. Halton camp was a revelation and a delight after Padgate. The brick barrack blocks of 5 Wing were warm and comfortable, well laid out around a parade ground with plenty of hot water, and with a mirror in the lobby to check one's appearance before going out. We were well fed in a proper, comfortable dining hall, which had only one drawback - we shared it with the cockroaches. The camp headquarters building was a former Rothschild mansion, of which there are several in that area - I have since visited both Waddesdon and Wing.

There was an airfield and an expanse of tree-lined playing fields. I played rugby - our coach was a former rugby league player. In the RAF we were all amateurs with none of that silly snobbery between the codes, which lasted for so long. I also played hockey, and took up boxing. At the medical examination on the day before the tournament, I was found to have German measles, so was I packed off to the famous Princess Mary's RAF Hospital at the top of the camp. I felt such a fraud, as I did not really seem to be ill.

We had elementary instruction in unarmed combat. There were church parades on the square where on one occasion the inspecting officer, Air Commodore Swann, Air Officer Commanding Halton, censured one man as needing a haircut, while his own long white hair disappeared beneath his collar. However, one does not expect justice, just the hope of sometimes 'getting away with it.'

Kit inspection was a weekly chore, with blankets and sheets neatly folded into a cube at the head of the bed, with one's kit laid out in the prescribed manner in front. Even the soles of our spare pair of boots were polished. Our blue canvas webbing harness, pack and water bottle cover were cleaned with a diluted blue paste, the RAF equivalent of Army 'Blanco', and all brassware - buttons, belt buckle, cap-badge webbing buckles - were polished with 'Brasso', later succeeded by 'Duraglit' wadding. On one occasion I was complimented on my kit by the inspecting officer. That did not endear me to my comrades. I received goodies from home - fruit cake and jars of Chinese preserved ginger in syrup, for example, whish shared with my books the limited spare room in my locker. More importantly, we were all there for a purpose.

The training workshops were across the main road from the domestic side, and we

23

marched there in large squads. In the dark a rearguard carried a red lantern. Halton had been founded by Trenchard for the training of aircraft apprentices, on courses of up to three years, to form the technical backbone of the RAF. They marched to the workshops twice daily, led by bands of varying competence. I can still hum their principal march tune. There were also the 'sea pigs', the Fleet Air Arm apprentices, who were receiving a similar training to the RAF apprentice.

My own training as a flight rigger lasted for five months, much shorter than that of the apprentices. We were the first men's course at Halton, a wartime expedient to provide a rapid increase in aircraft maintenance personnel. It was a new and hasty assembly of the essentials and was excellent. I and some others were straight from school; some had worked in garages or engineering factories. The course was divided into sections, each giving us part of the knowledge and the skills we would need for our job in the RAF. The main sections of instruction were:

1. 'Basic' which included the names, varieties and uses of tools; using tools to saw, file and drill metals; the use of taps and dies, of surface plates, V-blocks and dial-test indicators; the names and variations of aircraft standard parts such as nuts, screws, washers and bolts, split pins, taper pins, etc, and the making of a 'test piece' requiring the use of our recently acquired knowledge and skills. I could produce working drawings for that piece now. In fact I have done so and the drawing is included in this story.

2. Aircraft construction, assembly and dismantling; rigging biplanes, aerodynamics.

3. Wheels, tyres and brakes.

4. Hydraulics

5. Pneumatics

6. Woodwork for aircraft

7. Fabric aircraft covering and its repair.

8. Splicing Ropes and wire cables. For splicing steel cables one used a tool called an ice pick, which had a wooden handle and a long steel shaft with a hardened point. One day my ice pick slipped and went through the ball of my left thumb and through the nail. The sickbay fixed me up and I had no ill effects.

9. Aerodrome procedure: this part was held on the airfield and included ground handling and starting aircraft; ground signals area; a demonstration of parachute packing and, there being a conveniently suitable building, gas drill, including a run through a gas-filled room, to show us how nasty tear gas was without the mask. The perimeter of Halton aerodrome was littered with the remains of ancient relics such as the Fairey Gordon biplane used for instructional purposes and a 'Hucks' starter, designed many years before by one Hucks, famous in early flying history. I missed part of the aerodrome course when I was in bed with influenza.

At the end of the course I was examined by a group of Warrant Officers and Flight Sergeants, from the Central Trade Test

Training the 'Few'

Board at Uxbridge, who assessed my test piece, asked me to identify various aircraft parts drawn at random from a large box, and took me on an inquisitorial tour of an aeroplane. At the end I was told that I had done well, and was asked if I would like to be considered for pilot training. I explained that my defective eyesight precluded that. When the results were announced I found that I had passed out top of the entry, with 84.4%, and I was the only one promoted to Leading Aircraftman (on 6th March 1940). My pay rose from two shillings to five shillings a day. I was sent to the stores to be issued with a pair of the L.A.C. propeller arm badges, which I duly sewed on. When I entered the dining hall for tea, the duty sergeant shouted out 'make way for our new L.A.C.' How embarrassing!

That was the end of my time at Halton, and a very good time it was. There had been a very severe winter, several home visits, and a lot of fun. I was posted on 11th March 1940 to 19 Squadron at Duxford, near my home town of Cambridge, a doubly fortunate posting, being to a top-notch squadron and close to my home and to the support of my family.

These men and women, during this period were trained and expected to uphold the highest traditions of the Royal Air Force. When war did finally come, they did not falter in their roles as aircrew or ground staff personnel and to them, this country owes a debt of gratitude, which can be never be fulfilled.

CHAPTER 2

The Battle for France & the Low Countries

As the last few hours of peace ebbed away following Germany's invasion of Poland on 1st September 1939, and the British Government waited in hope for the reply that had been sent to Adolf Hitler to remove his forces back across the border; plans were being prepared by RAF Fighter Command's commander in chief Air Chief Marshal Sir Hugh Dowding to send four Hurricane squadrons to France in preparation, if war should break out.

At 11.15 am on the morning of 3rd September, Prime Minister Neville Chamberlain spoke over the radio to tell the British nation, that no reply to Britain's demand for Germany to retreat had been met. Therefore Britain and her allies were now at war.

Within days, four Hurricane squadrons consisting of Nos 1, 73, 85 and 87 were on their way to bases situated in Northern France as part of the Advanced Air Striking Force which also consisted of Bristol Blenheim and Fairey Battle light bomber squadrons in support of the British Expeditionary Force army who were being sent to reinforce the French.

During the first few weeks, there was little activity in the air or on the ground, as France and Britain prepared for Hitler's next move. What was he up to, after easily defeating the Polish army and air force? Occasionally, the RAF would sight German reconnaissance aircraft intruding into French airspace along the border, but there was very little in the way of combat; perhaps the odd skirmish.

This period of waiting, began to make the civilian population wonder if there really was a war going on and therefore it was labelled the 'Phoney War'. This carried on for several months. Pilot Officer Peter Ayerst of No.73 Squadron was one of the first pilots to be sent across the Channel to France during those early days of the war and he remembers this time and his first experience of meeting the enemy:

Battle for France and the Low Countries

We first went to Le Havre together with No. 1 Squadron and we were linked up with them the whole time we were there in France, up until we were ordered out. We formed the fighter element of the Advanced Air Striking Force; the other two squadrons 85 and 87 were up north behind the Belgian border and they were the fighter element of the Air Component. Although we were not on the same airfield as No. 1 Squadron, we were about forty miles away from each other; we used to link up in the air together and meet for social functions.

We were there for two weeks waiting for our ground staff to arrive by boat and once they had arrived and we were together as a full squadron, all camped under canvas. We were then moved forward to a place called 'Rouvres' which was situated between Verdun and Metz, we stayed there until 10th May, when the Germans began to overrun the low-countries.

We began to put up standing patrols immediately we arrived in that area south of Luxembourg; we flew in formations of three at twenty thousand feet up and down the French-German border, east of Metz and we used to stay up for an hour a time and then another lot would come up and we would go back; this went on, weather permitting all day. The Germans often came up to have a look at us; when we saw them we would go towards them and we would have a few combats along those patrol lines. My section leader at that time was a New Zealander named 'Cobber 'Kain who became the RAF's first ace of the war, he was quite experienced compared to myself.

I can remember my first combat, it was on 6th November 1939, and I was called to do a thing called aerodrome defence, where one pilot had to sit in his aircraft, strapped in ready to go if the word came through that the Germans were around. I was detailed to do this that day and it was around 2.30 pm that afternoon, when the airman in the ridge tent, which was our flight office shouted that the red flag was waving. We had some French soldiers in a ditch around one side of the airfield, who had a powerful pair of binoculars and if they saw an enemy aircraft approaching, they would give an early warning, which was waving a red flag. The flag was spotted and when I looked up there was an aircraft overhead at about 20,000 feet obviously taking photographs of our airfield and I immediately took off and climbed as fast as I could with full boost. I gradually gained height.

As I climbed up I could see the German in the distance and I was then at about 18,000 feet and was closing very slowly on him, when I noticed him starting to come down quite fast. It was almost impossible to catch him then. He flew into cloud and I never saw him again, I thought 'oh well' and I headed in a westerly direction and headed for home. I didn't have a clue where I was; but I was well into Germany by then and I didn't realise how far in. I turned again and soon after I sighted nine aircraft in line astern flying below me and in front. I assumed this was the RAF offensive patrol that had been designated to fly that day. I thought it was these chaps, so I decided to join up and fly back with them. As I got up close in line astern I noticed the huge black crosses, they were Messerschmitt 109s, so I pulled up and gave the aircraft at the tail-end a quick burst and down he spiralled.

Nine against one wasn't very good odds, so I dived down 5,000 feet where there was some broken cloud and moved in and out of it hoping to avoid the eight Germans who were now chasing after me. Unbeknown to me, there was another eighteen of them above, I didn't know that, but also what I didn't know was that the German pilots had been concentrating so much on me that they didn't look after their own backsides, that some French fighters, Moraine and Curtis Hawks which had been on patrol over the Maginot Line, had waded into the Germans and shot nine of them down out of the twenty-seven. It was the first big air battle of the war and I was dubbed 'decoy'.

I was getting short of fuel by this time, having been airborne for some time, so I thought I must find an airfield and get down somehow. I noticed some aircraft circling and I reckoned there must be an airfield nearby and there was. I landed and I was taxiing in when I got to the point that my engine cut out because I had run out of fuel. When I got back to my own airfield the following day, the flight engineer came over and said 'you know sir, you shouldn't have flown this aircraft back, and there a quite a few bullet holes in your tail-plane and some are a bit dicey. I said 'well at least I got it back, ignorance is bliss'. It was later claimed that I had shot down the first Messerschmitt 109 of the war.

Roger Morewood who had been flying Hawker Hurricanes at North Weald in Essex received orders to go to a new squadron:

I was posted away from 56 Squadron in October 39 to form a brand new squadron, No. 248. I thought this was terrific, a brand new fighter squadron and when I arrived at Hendon, what did I find 'Blenheims.'

We had masses of brand new pilots and most of them were quite green, they had only flown primitive aircraft and we all had to convert to twin engines. A chap named Arthur Pennington-Legh and I, the two flight commanders thought it was quite easy, but the brand new boys took a long time before we could become operational.

The Bristol Blenheim was alright to fly, it was a very pleasant aeroplane, it did what you wanted to do with it, docile, nice kindly aircraft, but it wasn't fast enough to catch the enemy or fast enough to get away.

I was sent on an operation with my brand new flight over to Den Helder in the Netherlands to guard a battleship, when I saw what I thought to be bomber aircraft coming up to attack. I got my boys into line astern formation and went into attack, but they weren't bombers at all, they were Messerschmitt 110s. My other two chaps disappeared into cloud and I was left in one of those unimaginable positions where you don't know what's going on, you just point your nose and fire at anything you can see, until I had run out of ammunition. I thought 'well I'm going home now' so off I set, my gunner in the back then told me we were going to be attacked from astern and we were. They ruined the aircraft, but I got it back to Bircham Newton, nobody hurt, nothing to laugh at. After this episode I think they realised how stupid it was sending us on escort over a battleship in Holland with Blenheims, we were then posted up to Dyce where we were up to our axles in mud when we landed.

Flying Officer John 'Killy' Kilmartin of No.1 Squadron was also sent to France and remembers his first impressions of the squadron's new base and the first contact with the enemy:

I found myself in France with No.1 Squadron and the conditions were pretty rough; bad enough for us, the officers, but ten times worse for the ordinary airmen who were sleeping in cowsheds and cattle barns. We were fairly comfortably billeted except we had to sleep on straw mattresses on the floor; it was as bad as that. The rations were pretty atrocious, Mr Macconnichies meat and veg and that sort of thing.

There was no such thing as Radar or navigation aids, just standing patrols. Occasionally we would get the odd German reconnaissance aircraft come over; and in fact the first bit of combat I

32

had was when three of us attacked a Dornier 17. My section was being led by a chap called 'Pussy' Foster. He got the first burst into this bomber and two of the crew baled out straight away, but the pilot stayed with the aircraft and glided it down to land. I was with a sergeant pilot named Soper and he and I had a bash at this thing as well. It didn't seem to make much difference as it kept on going with both engines out and gliding in. 'Pussy' flew up alongside the German who was flying quite slowly now, only just above stalling speed and flew immediately in front of the German, who immediately fired off his only forward firing gun and promptly shot poor old 'Pussy' down. He fortunately baled out.

Anyway this aircraft eventually crash-landed and the pilot who was a non-commissioned officer, his name was Frankenberger, he was picked up by the French and we asked if we could possibly see him. The French, who were quite reluctant, eventually agreed and brought him along to our mess. The German, he was terrified, he thought he was going to be thumped or given the third degree hammering. After a few whiskies, he mellowed up a bit and gave us all kinds of information. That was the first bit of combat that I had.

Sergeant William 'Taffy' Higginson of No. 56 Squadron based at North Weald remembers that while only a small contingent of RAF squadrons were in France, the ones left back in Britain had very little to do but carry out shipping convoy patrols in the Channel and over the North Sea.

Battle for France and the Low Countries

In January 1940, we were patrolling convoys off the east coast. We were invited to attend a convoy briefing and the person in charge introduced us to some of the captains of the vessels we would protect. One of the skippers asked a question, 'how big is your aircraft and how will we distinguish it from a German? This was an impossible question to answer, but I said 'if you take your box of matches and the aircraft exceeds the size, then you can assume that it is a German. The reply came, 'look here pilot, if you come anywhere near my vessel, we will bloody well shoot you down.' Fortunately, none of them ever did put that into practice.

'Killy' Kilmartin No. 1 Squadron

One of the early morning patrols was to patrol 15 miles inland between Luxembourg and the German border and when the patrol had finished I was the first to land and we couldn't get the petrol tankers up onto the field, so we had to taxi to the road and they would refuel. As I was the first in I was the first to be refuelled. As I taxied back to dispersal, I saw the contrails of an aircraft above and I immediately took off. Sure enough I climbed up and caught up with a German bomber, I thought it was a Heinkel at the time, because it had two engines and a single tail and Dorniers had two fins on the tail. It was behaving very oddly and as soon as it saw me it dived. This was at about 22,000 feet and I thought this is no Heinkel, they never travel this fast, but I

34

still didn't know what it was. We came down to tree-top height and he was firing at me and I at him and we both scored hits on each other. I eventually crash-landed in a field somewhere and he did the same further on. The aircraft turned out to be a Junkers 88 and I claimed it was the first Junkers 88 to be shot down in the war. The trouble was we didn't have any silhouettes of it, we had everything else. I was flying a fixed two blade Hurricane at the time and there was no means of controlling the engine speed in the dive and the engine was shaking so much that I thought it was going to jump out of its bearings, which gave you an idea of the speed we were going down at. It was well over 350 knots.

Shortly afterwards I got a replacement aircraft with a Rotal three-bladed constant speed propeller. It transformed the Hurricane and made it a much better fighter, before that it really wasn't of much use. Nice to fly, but that was about all, certainly not to go to war in. Johnny Walker was my flight commander in A Flight, 'Prosser' Hanks was B Flight commander, we had an Australian with us named Clisby, and he was killed out in France, as was a chap named Lorimar. Both Paul Ritchie and Billy Drake had been wounded and they were shipped back to Britain.

On 10th May 1940, Germany finally unleashed its Blitzkrieg attack, coming through the forests of the Belgian Ardennes, catching the Allies totally unaware and unprepared for the fast moving Panzer Tank Divisions and advanced Luftwaffe strikes, which overran every Allied position barring their way. Although the French and British Armies fought hard to stem the German advance and fighting was fierce in many places, it seemed almost impossible to launch any organised counter-attacks. Communication between the armies was fragmented and no sooner was a position set up to defend, the Germans had already by-passed it or it had been taken through force. Flying Officer Norman Hayes of No. 600 Squadron was at Manston aerodrome the day the Germans launched their offensive and remembers his squadron's mission that day:

> On 9th May, I had been on night duty and there had been a lot of night air activity over Holland, Belgium and the Channel, but personally I had not been involved in any interceptions, one of our chaps Mike Anderson had, with a German bomber of some sort. We all remained at readiness and at about midday we all piled into our cars and dashed to the mess to get a quick lunch. We had just arrived when suddenly somebody dashed out and told us that we were needed back at dispersal immediately. We rushed back and were met on arrival by section commander 'Grubby' Grice and he took us into the briefing room. I remember his first words 'You chaps have got a tough job, information has come through that the Germans have captured Waalhavent airfield at Rotterdam and you with six Blenheims are to fly over there engage any enemy aircraft over the airfield and if you don't see any aircraft, beat up the airfield.
>
> I flew as No. 2 to Jimmy Wells who led the operation with our six Blenheims; it was a lovely afternoon and you could see

the Dutch coast almost as you took off from Manston, a beautiful sunny day. As we approached we could see fires burning in the dock areas. Jimmy led us in and the only aircraft around were our own and he led us into attack. I followed Jimmy down and we all selected targets; the airfield was full of Junkers Ju52s and I think I shot up one or two of these. As I pulled away I could see Messerschmitt 110s coming down on our tails. I turned towards them and there was an awful mix up and we all broke up.

I never saw another Blenheim until I noticed one shooting up a Junkers 52, suddenly a 110 got onto his tail and that was the last I saw of him. I shot up another Ju52, but was then badly shot up myself, I had petrol pouring into the cockpit, the starboard tank had been pierced and I started to have trouble with the controls. In the heat of the moment I had to think of all the balance cocks to transfer fuel from one tank to another. I managed to keep my engines running, but since I was badly shot up I decided to get out as quickly as I could, so I dived down to ground-level and found out I was flying on a reciprocal course and heading in towards Germany. I turned around and as I came back I encountered lots of Heinkel 111s and I used up my ammunition on these chaps. I decided then to climb up, gain some height along the Dutch/ Belgian coast before crossing over to Manston.

When I got back to base I stopped my aircraft as soon as I landed and I was met by 'Grubby' Grice. I said to him 'How many of the chaps are back' he said 'You're the first' I said 'I'm sorry, but I don't think the others will come back' and of course none of them did. There was one chap who was quite badly hurt named Hugh Rowe, he was looked after by a Dutch doctor for some weeks before he was given up to the Germans and spent the remainder of the war as a prisoner. Another survivor was a fellow called Dick Haine who came back on the naval destroyer that carried Queen Wilhelmina and her family to safety. He and his gunner, Cramer both survived, but none of the others did unfortunately.

Sergeant Peter Morfill of 501 Squadron had flown to France from RAF Tangmere to support the RAF fighters already paying a heavy price in aircraft and men:

We were sent to France at a place called Bethenville which was north-east of Rheims. We had only been there a day, when the bombing started and other sorts of odd things. The place was a bit of a shambles as we had no ground control as we had in England, when we knew exactly what was happening.

Out there we had scrambled telephone messages and it was disorganised because we were being moved around so quickly from pillar to post. The Germans were advancing so rapidly. We would only stay on one aerodrome for maybe two days at the most.

On 15th May, British communications relayed the news that Holland had surrendered at 11.00 am following the devastation which befell the city of Rotterdam. 20,000 buildings had been laid waste by the German bombing and artillery and 1,000 civilians had lost their lives.

In France the situation worsened when German Panzers had broken through and taken the bridges over the Meuse River and at Sedan the front line had been breached and the Germans were now pouring through.

With many civilians packing the roads seeking refuge, re-enforcements were unable to travel and had to cut across the French countryside to try and get to suitable defensive positions. The advancing Germans had no such compassion and sent ahead their dreaded screaming Stuka dive-bombers and fighter aircraft to strafe the fleeing refugees who blocked the roads, causing them to jump into the side ditches to avoid bombs and bullets; many were slaughtered in this way.

Air Chief Marshal Sir Hugh Dowding's letter of 16th May 1940 to Prime Minister Winston Churchill advising him of the present state of RAF Fighter Command and the call not to send any further RAF aircraft to France.

Sir,

I have the honour to refer to the very serious calls which have recently been made upon the Home Defence Fighter Units in an attempt to stem the German invasion on the Continent.

2. I hope and believe that our Armies may yet be victorious in
France and Belgium, but we have to face the possibility that they may
be defeated.

3. In this case I presume that there is no one who will deny that England should fight on, even though the remainder of the Continent of Europe is dominated by the Germans.

4. For this purpose it is necessary to retain some minimum fighter strength in this country and I must request that the Air Council will inform me what they consider this

minimum strength to be, in order that I may make my dispositions accordingly.

5. I would remind the Air Council that the last estimate which was made as to the force necessary to defend this country was 52 Squadrons, and my strength has now been reduced to the equivalent of 36 Squadrons.

6. Once a decision has been reached as to the limit on which the Air Council and the Cabinet are prepared to stake the existence of the country, it should be clear to the Allied Commanders on the Continent that not a single aeroplane from Fighter Command beyond the limit, will be sent across the Channel, no matter how desperate the situation may become.

7. It will, of course be remembered that the estimate of 52 Squadrons was based on the assumption that the attack would come from the eastwards except in so far as the defences might be outflanked in flight. We have now to face the possibility that attacks may come from Spain or even from the North coast of France. The result is that our line is very much extended at the same time as our resources are reduced.

8. I must point out that within the last few days the equivalent of 10 Squadrons have been sent to France, that the Hurricane Squadrons remaining in this country are seriously depleted, and that the more Squadrons which are sent to France the higher will be the wastage and the more insistent the demands for reinforcements.

9. I therefore request that as a matter of paramount urgency the Air Council will consider and decide what level of strength is to be left to the Fighter Command for the defences of this country, and will assure me that when this level has been reached, not one fighter will be sent across the Channel however urgent and insistent the appeals for help may be.

Battle for France and the Low Countries

10. I believe that, if an adequate fighter force is kept in this country if the fleet remains in being, and the Home Forces are suitably organised to resist invasion, we should be able to carry on the war single handed for some time, if not indefinitely. But, if the Home Defence Force is drained away in desperate attempts to remedy the situation in France, defeat in France will involve the final, complete and irremediable defeat of this country.

I have the honour to be Sir,

Your Obedient Servant

H.T. Dowding
Air Chief Marshal
Air Officer Commanding-in-Chief
Fighter Command, Royal Air Force.

The battle raged on the ground and in the air, as the German advance continued and seemed unstoppable. No. 32 Squadron was now using Merville as their airfield. On 18th May, Flight Lieutenant Peter Brothers was in action leading B Flight, when he claimed his second German aircraft destroyed near Le Cateau at midday.

> The visibility that day was good with a slight haze up to 9,000 feet. I saw Green Section engage 12 Messerschmitt 109s astern of me, so I turned and flew towards them. Three 109s flew over me in line astern, so I turned sharp left as they dived on my tail. As they turned away and as I was turning, a 109 flew directly across my sights. I gave him a short burst of fire and he slowly turned on his back and dived inverted at about 45 degrees. I followed him down, but he gained speed and remained inverted.

41

Battle for France and the Low Countries

> I looked around and suddenly saw another 109 on my tail. I turned steeply to the left and he opened fire with tracer ammunition. His shooting was hopeless and I saw it pass behind me. I turned on to his tail, but as I fired, he dived into cloud and I lost him. I circled round, but all the aircraft appeared to have gone home, so after a few minutes I returned to Merville. I noticed that the north-west of Cambrai was burning furiously.

Elements of the German 1st Panzer Division had reached the French coast by 19th May. General Gort commander of the British Expeditionary Force no longer thought the battle to defend France was possible and in a message to the War Office on 19th May concluded that if possible the Army must be evacuated, before all was lost.

On 20th May, Vice Admiral Sir Bertram Ramsey, a Flag Officer Commanding Dover, was charged with the task of organising a possible evacuation of the British Expeditionary Force under the code-name Dynamo, as the army retreated towards the Channel ports.

Operation Dynamo was implemented between 6 pm and 7 pm on Sunday 26th, when every available ship and boat was ordered to head for the Dunkirk area. During the proceeding week many men had already been evacuated from Boulogne and Calais, where fierce fighting took place between the 19th and 26th.

By Monday 27th May, Dynamo was in full operation and the scores of 'Little Ships' were making many trips to and fro across the Channel. The armies on the beaches continued bravely to endure the Luftwaffe bombing, while patiently waiting their turn in the long queues to get aboard a ship and home to safety.

Pilot Officer Alan Deere of 54 Squadron would later reflect on those early patrols over the Dunkirk beach-head, which for many young pilots would be their baptism of fire:

Battle for France and the Low Countries

When the British Army started retreating and Dunkirk was going to be the point of evacuation, fighter squadrons from East Anglia as well as from 11 Group were sent to patrol to cover the beaches and we did two or three trips a day. It was the first time we fighter pilots had crossed the Channel to undertake combat and then come back.

The endurance factor of the Spitfire at that time was fairly critical; you couldn't stay too long, and we weren't accustomed to finding our way back so to speak; and so we patrolled the coast from Boulogne up to Dunkirk and up as far as Antwerp trying to support the British army on the ground.

We met the Germans in combat; they had moved some of their bases forward and they were able to get their fighters as far as the bridgehead. We came into contact for the first time with Dornier, Heinkels and Messerschmitt 110s and 109s.

Fighter Command Headquarters decided to try using the squadrons over Dunkirk in larger formations on 28th May, which might have more impact against the big German formations of escort fighters. Unfortunately due to the thundery cloud conditions and poor visibility, the RAF squadrons soon lost contact with one another.
'Taffy' Higginson flying with 56 Squadron would later recall his memories of Dunkirk:

Dunkirk was an extraordinary operation, people leaving by all means available, small boats and big ships. On some occasions there were no aircraft in the sky and other cases the sky seemed as if it was full of aeroplanes. When patrolling Dunkirk, what we did was to fly over the beach, we did a few circuits around and either got into combat with the enemy or met nothing. At this time the Germans were advancing down through France and to some extent it was far more important for them than the evacuation of Dunkirk. A lot of their aircraft were moving with the front line down to the Somme towards Abbeville and other areas.

The RAF had a limited number of aircraft and my logbook shows later on that we were still doing sweeps over to Amien and Rouen escorting bombers in May and the beginning of June; there wasn't enough aircraft to give complete protection. I think they did jolly well, when you consider that as far as I could see they had little or no other means of defence. They could put up very little resistance.

By 31st May, over 194,600 Allied troops had been taken off the beaches, which was a miracle in itself. German artillery, which had been moved up, was now targeted on the beachhead.

The operation continued however, till 4th June, when the last ships left Dunkirk at about 3.40 pm. Shortly afterwards the town and beaches fell to the Germans. Percy Morfill of 501 Squadron was given orders with the rest of his colleagues to try and make their own way back to Britain:

During the withdrawal from France, I managed to get as far as Guernsey, my Hawker Hurricane had been damaged in the wing tanks by enemy fire and I couldn't get back to the mainland; so on landing I burnt the aircraft and came back to England on a fishing boat with a couple of other chaps left in the same position.

Sergeant Pilot Desmond Fopp serving with No. 17 Squadron also remembers his final days in France:

Before leaving Le Mans because of the German advance, we discovered that the army had left a pool of motorbikes, many of which were in running order, so the whole squadron turned out in force and we had a hair- raising race around the Le Mans circuit before destroying the whole lot. We also found that the NAAFI had evacuated leaving all of the stores behind, so we decided to fill our kit bags with cigarettes and booze before destroying the remainder of the goods. We then proceeded to Dinard, which is not far from Cherbourg on the coast. We stayed there for one week and then retreated to Jersey and then Guernsey, where we spent one night as it was decided that the Channel Islands should be left to the Germans to avoid mass bombing of the civilian population.

During this evacuation from France, it was either a case of either find an aircraft to fly or remain and hope to get to St. Nazaire and get a boat to England. It was amazing how some people came back.

We had three pilots return in a Fairey Battle aircraft which had no flaps and had to be flown with the wheels down. Another two chaps returned in a light aircraft named a Magister and another couple came back in a Hurricane sitting

45

on the lap of the other. Personally I brought my Hurricane back with a flat tail-wheel tyre, no brakes and no ammunition.

When we arrived back at Tangmere, we were given seven days leave; and I returned home to be greeted by my grandmother who asked 'Where have you been? You are dirty and untidy. Have you deserted? But she was most grateful for some of the cigarettes in my kit bag!

Pilot Officer Peter Dawburn was just nineteen years old; he served in the same squadron as Desmond Fopp, No.17. He too recalls those urgent times as the squadron prepared to withdraw from France and what action he had to take to return to Britain:

I was preparing to get into my Hurricane to fly back to England, when my flight commander came up to me and said 'I'm taking your aircraft, mine is unserviceable, you'll have to find your own way back' I couldn't believe it, I thought what am I going to do now?. I started walking back and as I passed one of the hangars there was an engine fitter working on a Fairey Battle aeroplane. I asked him 'does it fly? And he replied 'Yes, but it doesn't have any hydraulics to work the brakes or flaps. I replied I would take it and I asked him if he wished to come along as a passenger, he replied 'Not likely.'

He helped me push the kite on to the airfield and I prepared to take off. I hadn't even got a map, but I knew where north was and took off. I crossed the Channel and landed at Exeter Airport, which was by sheer luck, rather than judgement. The landing was pretty dodgy due to having no brakes to slow the machine down; and I managed to stop just a few inches from the boundary hedge.

Thankful to have landed back in good old England, I walked over to the control tower and was met by a chap named John Cunningham, later to be known as the night-fighter ace 'Cat's Eyes.' He said 'What the bloody hell are you doing here? I explained who I was and where I had flown from. He kindly organised for me to borrow a Tiger Moth biplane to fly back to my squadron's home base at Debden.

Pilot Officer Bob Foster

When I arrived at 605 Squadron the commanding officer was Walter Churchill, he had served in France and had been very successful and had been awarded a DSO and a DFC, the only man to get that as far as I know in France. The squadron had been clobbered over Dunkirk and they had lost their commanding officer and the losses were filled by regulars and VRs. The first ones in were the regulars like Christopher 'Bunny' Currant, Michael Cooper-Slipper and Jock Muirhead was another, so by the time I joined them up at Drem on 6th June, there were only about five auxiliaries left of the original squadron.

The final result of the evacuation had seen the rescue of 338,226 Allied servicemen, which would have resulted in the loss of so many soldiers that it would have been doubtful whether Britain could have resisted an invasion if it had come and might have seen this country call for peace terms. Although Dunkirk and the fall of France were seen as a devastating defeat, the spirit of the British people was still unvanquished. Winston Churchill in his speech in the House of Commons on 18th June 1940 declared that Britain was now alone in the struggle against the Nazis. He went on to say:

> 'What General Weygand called the Battle of France is over. I expect that the Battle of Britain is about to begin. The whole fury and might of the enemy must very soon be turned on us. Hitler knows that he will have to break us in this island or lose the war.
>
> If we can stand up to him, all of Europe may be free and the life of the world may move forward to broad sunlit lands. But if we fail, then the whole world including the United States, including all we have known and cared for, will sink into the abyss of a new Dark Age made more sinister and perhaps more protracted by the lights of perverted science.
>
> Let us therefore brace ourselves to our duties and so bear ourselves that, if the British Empire and its Commonwealth last for a thousand years, men will still say 'This was their finest hour'.

The people of Britain now watched and waited with bated breath as to whether they could defend their island from possibly an immediate invasion from Hitler's victorious armies and air forces now in command along the French coast. The next few weeks would surely tell.

CHAPTER 3

Operational Training Units

Before the outbreak of the Second World War most pilots who joined their new squadrons were totally unaware as to the tactics used in aerial combat or the experience needed in firing an aerial gun. Any training was left to those older officers who had flown and fought during the First World War; or by the use of an Air Ministry hand book with outdated formation attacks and manoeuvres from the previous conflict.

Now that the Royal Air Force had the latest eight-gun monoplane fighter aircraft with speeds over 300 mph, new training methods had to be developed. At first Fighter Command Group Pools were organised and then later new Operational Training Units were formed precisely to train pilots on the aircraft that they would fly operationally once they were posted to a squadron.

When France fell in June 1940, many pilots who had fought and gained valuable experience flying combat against the Luftwaffe, were not sent back to their squadrons, but posted as new instructors to the Operational Training Units; here to educate the young pilots in the art of handling their aircraft and gain experience and confidence, to fly in formations and if lucky to get some air-firing at air or ground targets. This chapter charts the work of some of the operational training units with the accounts told by those who instructed and those who went to learn.

Peter Ayerst had seen action with No. 73 Squadron during the battle to save France in May 1940. After making his way back to England, he and his fellow squadron colleagues were in need of rest, but on arriving back at their base at Digby they were soon to be contacted by the powers that be for further deployment. Peter recalls the role he was to embark upon as an instructor:

> After we had arrived back from France, we all re-mustered back at Digby and a few weeks later the Air Officer Commander of

Operational Training Units

12 Group, Trafford Leigh-Mallory came and saw us and talked with us, he said 'I suppose you would like a spot of leave' and we said 'yes please'. He said 'You can have four days, because I want you back, we have some units which are fairly new, called Operational Training Units, we have two at the moment, one at Sutton Bridge near Kings Lynn and one at Aston Down, Gloucester. You will be going as instructors.'

Most of us 73 Squadron chaps went to Sutton Bridge and we were quite busy down there instructing new pupils coming through, with what we had learnt with tactics and formations and so on. I suppose after about three weeks I was called and told I was going to be posted. They were starting up a new OTU with Spitfires, because the other two units which were in existence only had Hurricanes, so with more Spitfires coming, they had to have a Spitfire OTU. They took some of the chaps from Sutton Bridge and Aston Down to form the nucleus of instructors at No. 7 OTU Hawarden near Chester and that's where I first flew a Spitfire. We were thrown straight in, because we had gained more experience than anybody else, having been in France for eight or nine months, so we were the ones that had to impart our knowledge.

After one flight in a Spitfire, I was then teaching the new pilots the formations in Spitfires and the tactics, but on the other hand I had a lot of experience on the Hurricane. In edition to teaching the pilots, we as instructors had also had to do readiness and patrols over Liverpool and

Manchester. I stayed there for about six or seven months.

We had Miles Master aircraft, a two seat monoplane trainer and we would take them up in the Master to give them some idea about what you could do in a Spitfire, I'd take off and tell them what they would have to look for, because the Spitfire had a narrow undercarriage, small wheels and tended to be nose heavy, so we tried to tell them all these things and show them. After one or two trips in the Master, we would then give them an entire briefing of the cockpit of the Spitfire, what to do and what to be careful of and gradually they flew the Spitfire.

As they gained confidence, we gradually taught them the fighter formations we had been using. They would also do a bit of air to ground firing, but during the early part of the course in the period of July and August, they were only there for about two weeks at the most, because the squadrons wanted pilots so urgently that we couldn't keep them any longer.

When we first started teaching the new pilots about tactics and formations, we were still really flying in formations of three aircraft, but later on as the Battle of Britain progressed, we started to fly in pairs and fours, which was a much more manoeuvrable type of formation.

We as instructors flew aircraft that were armed up, but the pupils were not. This did prove to be invaluable because on the 14th August, a single German bomber suddenly appeared out of the clouds and started bombing RAF Sealand which was only about five miles from us and we could hear the bombs exploding in the distance, so three of us dashed out and took off and went after this chap. We caught up with the German, which turned out to be a Heinkel 111, my other two friends went in first and sprayed him with bullets and then I went in a gave him a couple of bursts. We didn't destroy him, but he made a very good crash-landing in a field and the crew were taken prisoners; forty-six years later I met up with the German crew, when I was invited over to Germany.

There were a few accidents, but not too many. We were very close to the Welsh mountains and if the weather was some times bad, they would come down and forget about the mountains and crash into the side of the hills. We lost two of our pupils that way.

We had a lot of chaps from the Commonwealth countries, New Zealanders, Australians and a hell of a lot of Canadians. The Poles had there own instructors.

During this time I also instructed three American volunteers, they came over to help Britain during its time of need and they did very well. Sadly all three were killed later on in the war, but while they were at the OTU they did very well. One was named 'Shorty' Keough, he had been a professional parachutist and he had done around four hundred jumps, he was only about five feet high and we had to use cushions to help him see over the cockpit windscreen. Another was 'Red' Tobin, he was about six foot three and the other was 'Duke' Mamedoff, who was of average size. They had all flown previously as crop sprayers in the United States.

Operational Training Units

Looking back seventy years, I think bearing in mind we were instructing and we were trying to get these chaps operational as soon as possible, so they could go and join a squadron and not be a total cabbage, and they could soon be incorporated into the squadron operational scheme. In hindsight, we did a good job. If we had had more time, the training, it could have been improved; but as we were running so short of pilots they accepted anything they were given.

John 'Killy' Kilmartin had been in France with No.1 Squadron.

Once we had been kicked out of France, most of No.1 Squadron were sent as instructors to No. 5 OTU at Aston Down in Gloucester; Johnny Walker, 'Prosser' Hanks, 'Boy' Mould all went there with me.

Bob Foster who at that time was a sergeant pilot, recalls the operational training unit he was sent to in June 1940 to convert to Hurricane fighters

I was sent to No. 6 OTU at Sutton Bridge, near King's Lynn on the east coast to learn to fly the Hurricane. I was given a manual to look at then stuck in the cockpit and then the instructor lent over the side and more or less said 'push this, that and the other'. My instructor was a chap called Flying Officer Denis Smallwood who had been in France and had seen a certain amount of action and had some experience of air-fighting; he later became an air chief marshal.

I found the Hurricane very nice to fly; but we didn't know anything better in those days, having flown Hawker Harts, Audax's and the like. We did a certain amount of formation flying in Vic's, but that is about as much as we got; we did do some dog-fighting practice with our instructors and some air-firing on drogues a few times and that was the sum of our training. The guns were set for a range of three hundred yards, although later some of the pilots changed this to two-hundred.

After about forty hours I was posted to No. 605 Auxiliary Squadron which was based up at Drem in Scotland, which was a lucky posting because if I had been sent south to either Kenley or whatever into 11 Group with only about 40 hours on Hurricanes, and this is what happened to a lot of chaps; I think they suffered because of the lack of hours; they could fly the aircraft, but that is all they could do, as where I went up to Drem with 605 and stayed up there until September, by which time I had amassed 80-hours on type, which made a lot of difference. The more you fly the better you are and the more confident you are. So from my point of view it was a good posting.

Pilot Officer Richard Jones was sent to No. 5 OTU at Aston Down in early July 1940, learning to fly on the early Spitfire Mk 1s.

We had the early Spitfires which were fitted with a pump up handle undercarriage; the later Spitfires had an automatic undercarriage. Once you were airborne you had to change your hand over on the control stick then manually pump up the wheels. Those watching from the ground could see those pilots who had not got the hang of this manoeuvre, as the Spitfire would seem to be bouncing up and down once airborne until the wheels finally retracted. We also had to fix the propeller either in fine or course. We didn't have the constant speed propellers.

Les Harvey, a new sergeant pilot had spent one week at Aston Down at the beginning of August.

> I flew the Spitfire for the first three days and then swapped over and for the remaining four days flew the Hurricane. One incident which I was involved during that week and only due to pure luck, was when we were told to take off in a formation of three and by chance my original position as the left hand aircraft was changed over to the right. On our return to the airfield, a disastrous accident unfolded.
>
> A Bristol Blenheim twin-engine aircraft was taxing down the flight path to take-off, totally unaware of our formation coming in. We had not received any information and without warning the Hurricane flown by a chap named Jenkins, who had taken my original position collided head on with the Blenheim. The Hurricane went straight through the canopy of the Blenheim decapitating both the pilot and pupil. The Blenheim was up on its nose on fire and the Hurricane was lying in pieces with Jenkins dead. I had only been speaking to him a few minutes earlier just before the flight. It was pure chance, we had changed over, and it could have been me instead of him.
>
> I was only there for one week and I was a pall bearer three times during that period. I always remember just before leaving Aston Down, the commanding officer there who was a chap by the name of 'Bull' Hallahan, he had commanded No. 1 Squadron in

Operational Training Units

France, he said to us all 'I am sorry gentleman you have had such a short time here, but I would say to you, don't worry too much when you get to an operational squadron, survive this place, you will survive any operational squadron.' This was indeed true because the amount of crashes and that sort of thing was unbelievable; people were going through stone walls, undershooting and overshooting the runways.

Les was posted to Hornchurch, to 54 Squadron on the 22nd August to replace the casualties that the squadron had suffered during that month. On arrival, he was met by one of the flight commanders, a New Zealander Alan Deere. Les recalls what happened next.

Al Deere approached me and introduced himself and said to me, what time have you got on Spitfires? I said 'about four hours and twenty minutes and four hours on the Hurricane.' 'Oh, he said, that's useless, I don't know why they bothered to send you here we haven't got time to train you and we are far too busy', so he arranged to have me sent back to the operational training unit at Aston Down for another week.

Jimmy Corbin had finished his flying training at Kinloss and on 10th August was sent to No. 7 OTU at Hawarden for conversion on to Spitfires.

When you get to an OTU you are there for one purpose, to learn to fly whatever aircraft there is. In my case it was a Spitfire. I was only at the OTU for twelve days, during which time I did 29-hours flying on a Spitfire. When you get to a squadron you are not considered operational, you have got to

56

get used to the squadron procedure, which took a week to a fortnight. I have still got a copy of my aircraft manual which I pinched, because it was top secret in those days. You just arrived and you had a chap who had been flying spitfires for some time, I wouldn't call him an instructor, he was just someone who could fly Spitfires. You got into the aircraft and sat down and he would point out all the instruments to you. Then there came a day, one or two days in my case, when I was told 'Right Corbin, get in you're off'.

The Spitfire is a lovely aircraft, but it wasn't designed to stay on the ground. You have bugger-all view forward because of the big engine sticking out front, you had to zig zag to see what was in front of you. The undercarriage was comparatively narrow, so it wasn't a good aircraft on the ground. My first flight was bloody frightening to start off with, because you've got so much power. You start off flying with ordinary aircraft of about 250-hp then progress to over 1200 hp. Frightening, but then you realise afterwards that with experience your confidence grows, that is what it basically comes down to.

Official records show that during August the OTU's managed to turn out just over 250 pilots ready to take up the fight in operational squadrons, this however was not keeping up with the mounting casualties being suffered on a day-to-day basis down in the south-east; which in the same month had topped 300.

While the Battle of Britain raged on in the south of England, No. 7 OTU at Hawarden in Cheshire claimed another victim on 7th September, when instructor Sergeant L.S. Pilkington was going through the procedure of showing a pupil formation flying, when he heard over his headphones that an enemy aircraft had been sighted approaching Hoylake. He cut his lesson short and told the young pilot to return back to base, while he went to investigate. He sighted the lone Junkers Ju88 at 20,000 feet and went into the attack. He fired off his ammunition and then returned to base. Later that day, it was confirmed that the Ju88 he had attacked had crashed in Wales.

There is no doubt that without the incredible work done by the OTU's in keeping the supply of eager new fighter pilots coming, Fighter Command would have never been able to make up the loss rate, and although there was never a shortage of aircraft coming from the factories, thanks to the work and industrial planning of Lord Beaverbrook, there would have been Spitfires and Hurricanes, but no pilots to fly them and the battle would have been lost.

CHAPTER 4

Don't forget the Erk's Sir!

Over the last seventy years since the Battle of Britain, so much has been written about the role of those gallant airmen who defended our skies from the Nazi hoards during the summer of 1940, but very little has ever been told of those who served as technical staff and being of equal importance and whom without, the battle could have been lost. Those of whom I speak were the ground crews whose job it was to keep the fighter aircraft maintained and in tip top condition for the next following sortie into combat.

For every pilot and Spitfire or Hurricane there was a team of at least six ground crew. The team consisted of an airframe rigger, an engine fitter, a wireless engineer, armourers and any other willing body who was available in times of emergency.

Their day usually started an hour before dawn, rolling out the aircraft from hangars or preparing the ones already at the dispersal pens by warming the engines up, ready for the pilots to undertake the first patrol of the day.

The rigger was in charge of the aircrafts fuselage and wings; checking everything was in full working order, including flying controls, before allowing the aircraft to fly. The engine fitter would be responsible for the Rolls Royce Merlin engine, checking that there were no oil or glycol leaks or damage caused by previous combat. The Wireless engineer would check the TR9 wireless communications which allowed contact between pilot and Ops Room, vital once the pilot was airborne, so he could be guided from the ground and sent to the height and area where the enemy was to be engaged. He would also check the IFF instrument which gave out a signal defining the aircraft as friendly. While all this work was being seen too, the armourers would be hastily checking the machine guns in each wing, checking the breeches for bullet jams, cleaning the barrels and replenishing the ammunition with new belts of 0.303 bullets.

Once completed the machine guns were taped over with red tape linen, as not to allow any dirt or oil into the barrels before firing. The oxygen bottle situated behind the pilot's seat would be removed and replaced with a fresh one. Fresh aviation fuel would be brought up by a bowser and then pumped into the fuel tank, which was situated a few feet along the nose of the aircraft, just in front of the cockpit. Once everything had been completed the aircraft was signed off on Form 700.

John Milne served with No. 19 Squadron who were based at RAF Duxford, Cambridgeshire during the battle. He remembers his time and the role he and his colleagues played in keeping the squadron operational.

> I travelled to Duxford via Whittlesford Station: the main road at that time passed over the railway on a level crossing, next to the Red Lion. I slept at first on a 'let-down' metal bed in a crew-room off the hangar. Then I transferred to a ground-floor room in a barrack-block (not occupied by 19 Squadron) where I awoke one morning to find my trousers gone. Most of us had only one uniform. I waited until all those awake had left the room; I then stole another man's trousers. I wonder how the episode finished! Soon I transferred to a 19 Squadron room on the first floor of another block, and things were much better. We kept the room immaculately clean and tidy - the men were all regular airmen and well practiced in the domestic side of service life. The standard of 'Bullshit' was just like Halton: and when the floor had been polished with the 'bumper' (a heavily weighted felt pad on a pole) we moved around the room in our socks or on felt pads under both feet. I was introduced to snooker, played upstairs above the NAAFI (canteen) and a most popular pastime.
>
> Every morning we marched off to the hangar under the senior airman present, and pulled the Spitfires from the hangar and every night we moved them back in again. Soon they were

The young Lions. A group of new RAFVR trainees pictured at No. 4 E & RTS Brough in 1938. Those identified who flew during the Battle of Britain are, right to left back row: Ralph Havercroft, David Cox & Ronald Berry. Front row, from right, Stanley Andrews killed 11.9.40, 2nd right; John Ramshaw killed 4.9.40, others not known. (Courtesy of Mrs Jess Berryman)

Pre-war two-bladed Hawker Hurricane Mk1s of No. 56 Squadron based at NorthWeald, Essex, flying in line abreast formation.

(Courtesy of W/Cdr Roger Morewood)

Pilot Officer Peter Ayerst pictured on right with fellow pilot Derek Ford at No.12 Flying Training School at Grantham, Lincolnshire in 1938.

(Copyright W/Cdr Peter Ayerst)

Adolf Hitler greets Reichsmarschall Herman Goring, Commander in Chief of the Luftwaffe. It was Goring who promised Hitler that he could destroy RAF Fighter Command and make the German invasion of Britain possible without enemy opposition from the air. (Authors Collection)

Air Chief Marshal Sir Hugh Dowding, Commander-in-Chief of RAF Fighter Command between 1936-1940. It was he above all others that championed the use of early radar warning as a defensive system.

(Copyright IWM D 1417)

The RAF's first ace pilot of the war was Flying Officer Edgar 'Cobber' Kain DFC, a New Zealander serving with 73 Squadron.

(Copyright W/Cdr Peter Ayerst)

Pilots of No.73 Squadron relax at their officers' mess at Le Havre, September 1939. From left to right: F/Lt Bill Kain, F/O Peter Walker, P/O Peter Ayerst, F/O 'Fanny' Orton, P/O Claude Wright.

(Copyright W/Cdr Peter Ayerst)

A 501 Squadron Hurricane Mk1 being prepared and re-fuelled at its base at Betheniville following a recent sortie on 12th May 1940. (Copyright IWM C 1684)

This Heinkel He111 bomber was shot down on 19th June 1940 and crashed into the sea off an east coast beach. One of its crew baled out and his parachute became entangled with the aircraft's tail and he was strangled. The remains of the aircraft was hauled ashore; airmen are seen examining the parachute harness of the unfortunate German. (Authors Collection)

Flight Lieutenant Roger Morewood who helped form No.248 Squadron and later became their commanding officer in 1941.

(Courtesy of W/Cdr Roger Morewood)

A Bristol Blenheim of No.248 Squadron undertaking a reconnaissance patrol over the North Sea between the Netherlands and Norway. (Courtesy of W/Cdr Roger Morewood)

RAF ground personnel of Barrage Balloon Command prepare to launch another balloon into the air to provide protection against low-flying German aircraft over airfields, factories and other areas of strategic importance. (Copyright IWM CH 1519)

L.A.C's Len Davies & Bill Peacock after receiving their wings in June 1940, Davies was posted to No. 151 Squadron, while Peacock went to No. 46. Peacock was listed as missing in action on 11th September, when he failed to return from combat over the Thames Estuary in Hurricane V7232. (Courtesy of Len Davies)

Sergeant Robert William Foster pictured here before being commissioned to the rank of pilot officer and posted to No.605 Auxiliary Squadron based at Drem on 6th July 1940. (Courtesy of W/Cdr R. Foster DFC)

Adolf Hitler pictured at the Berghoff in July 1940 discussing plans for 'Operation Sealion' with Admiral Erich Raeder. Other present include from left to right: Field Marshal Walther von Brauchitsch, General Alfred Jodl, Field Marshal Wilhelm Keital and an unidentified Kriegsmarine staff officer. (Copyright IWM HU 75542)

Pilots of No. 65 Squadron try to relax outside their dispersal hut before the next sortie. Anytime, the scramble bell could ring and send them racing to their aircraft to intercept the next enemy raid. (Authors Collection)

Flight Rigger John Milne who served at Fowlmere & Duxford in 1940 with No. 19 Squadron. He was one of the many unsung heroes of the battle that serviced the aircraft from day to day. (Courtesy of John Milne)

Spitfires take to the air from Hornchurch, while others are worked on and prepared by their ground crews. (Copyright IWM 54411)

WAAFs prepare to undertake their next shift in the aerodromes operations room. They can be seen prepared with steel helmets in case of attack by the Luftwaffe. (Authors Collection)

One of the severely damaged aircraft hangars at RAF Manston following the attack by German bombers on 12th August. Note the workmen preparing to undertake repairs.

(Courtesy of the late S/Ldr E.D. Glaser)

All eyes are on the Plotting Board as WAAF's move position counters around the operations room map table as information is gathered on incoming German aircraft formations.
(Crown Copyright C1870)

A crashed Heinkel He111 bomber of III/KG27 lies by the side of the road at Charterhouse, Somerset, having been shot down at 6.00 pm on 14th August by Blue Section of No. 92 Squadron, who were based at Pembury, Carmarthenshire.
(Copyright IWM CH 1887)

F/Lt Peter Brothers of 32 Squadron pictured as the iconic portrait of an RAF Fighter pilot. (Authors collection)

moved permanently to a dispersal area around the south west side of the airfield, and we had a prefabricated hut to use as a crew-room by day and by night.

The war seemed at first to be remote and we routinely carried out the daily and periodic inspections of the aircraft, and performed all the incidental duties involved in servicing the aircraft and attending their take-offs and landings. An exhilarating duty was lying across the tail-plane, breathless, while the pilot ran the engine at high revs.

The Spitfire airframe and its installations and equipment, they came under the care of a flight rigger, were not difficult to repair and maintain. The Merlin engine, with its accessories, was, I think a bit more temperamental, particularly as regards oil and coolant leaks and loss of revs. A crew of rigger and mechanic looked after each aircraft, or sometimes two. Various specialist tradesmen - electricians, wireless mechanics, instrument repairers, and armourer's would appear, fiddle with their allotted bits and pieces, and then disappear. Wireless testing on the ground would go thus:

'Hello Dory, hello Dory, five three calling and testing, are you receiving me, are you receiving me, over.'

'Hello five three, hello five three, am receiving you loud and clear strength nine, over and out.'

The armourer's job could be arduous: ammunition is heavy, and loading the guns, with them and their ammunition tightly packed in the thin wings, was hard on the hands. When the guns had been fired, the riggers pasted squares of aircraft linen over the holes, giving a row of four square red patches at the leading edge of each wing. These patches maintained the smooth shape of the wing leading edge, essential to peak performance; and also prevented the guns from becoming colder and jamming through freezing. Starting the engine on an early Spitfire involved using a 'Trolley-Ac', a two-wheeled enclosed low hand-cart containing accumulators. One starter trolley was shared between several aircraft, so the crews became adept at high-speed trolley-pulling from one Spitfire to the next. Later Spitfires had Koffman cartridge starters, thus eliminating the 'Trolley-Ac' performance. The 'Trolley-Ac' had a thick electrical cable which plugged in through a flap in the engine-cowling. Once the engine had started, one of the crew pulled the cable out and took it away, being careful not to step back into the propeller! After starting the engine, the pilot would signal the ground crew to lie on the tail-plane while he ran the engine at high speed. This really took one's breath away.

After 'chocks away' the two-crew would take the wingtips and see the aircraft away from its parking area, until waved away by the pilot. Wheel chocks were originally individual items, with a man each to pull a rope which was so wrapped around the chock as to swivel it away from under the wheel and prevent it from jamming. The later system was to have both chocks connected by a steel angle iron, which enabled the pair of ground crew to execute a co-ordinated and speeded-up chock removal action.

A feature of the Spitfire design was the narrow wheel-track, dictated by the wing design. This did not make for stability in a rough landing, but the pilots just had to put up with it. Many Spitfires required wingtip repairs after tipping over in bumpy landings. An arduous job was pumping up the oleo legs - the undercarriage. It was not the pumping that was hard, but dragging the heavy equipment around the airfield. It consisted of a long vertical pump arm, a pump and a pressure-gauge to check the air pressure in the leg, all mounted on a large and heavy plank of wood, just like a railway sleeper.

One needed a strong back to service the Spitfire. The daily inspection included lifting the tail with one's back under the tail-plane, to check the tail wheel's functioning, and also similarly lifting each main plane in turn, beside the undercarriage attachment, to check the pintle bolt (holding the leg to the wing-spar) by its creaking or silence when dropped again. Some jobs were more complicated: one I remember was changing a stern-frame (the whole tail) in the hangar at Duxford.

No.19 Squadron moved to Fowlmere, back to Duxford, and eventually settled at Fowlmere. When we first moved to Fowlmere, there was no permanent accommodation. We slept in bell tents, feet to the central pole. A mobile cookhouse accompanied us - one day it caught fire! We dug latrine trenches and spent most of our time out of doors. Nobody seemed to mind. Fowlmere later had Nissen huts, never popular, as condensation dripped down from the underside of the cold steel roof onto one's bedding and oneself.

Flying from Fowlmere must have been fun! The airfield was far from level, and dipped down considerably in the corner nearest to Duxford. Part of it was laid with metal mesh decking to improve the surface. There were certain features of Duxford and Fowlmere which must remain forever recallable by everyone: the sound of Merlin engines starting, taxiing and flying low over the airfield; the smell of glycol coolant leaking on to hot metal; the smell of 100 octane petrol, and the staining from its green dye.

On 29 July 1940, I bought a motorcycle from King and Harper in Cambridge. It was a Royal Enfield 350 cc trials model, with knobbly tyres and a steel plate under the sump. I rode it home from the garage to show my parents and then to Duxford. I had hardly entered Duxford when I was told to paint over the shining aluminum mudguards with green camouflage paint!

19 Squadron operated for a time from Horsham St. Faith on the outskirts of Norwich, which was under construction as a permanent RAF Station. There were no hangars, workshops or living accommodation available, so the crews stayed for short tours in a hutted camp at Old Catton, Norwich, whence we travelled to and from Horsham St. Faith by lorry. Whilst there, I saw my first Cierva Autogyro, a primitive helicopter design.

The girls used to stand in the road outside the airfield and watch us, but we mostly ignored them, preferring to spend our time and money in the pub and cinema.

During one tour at Fowlmere, 'B' Flight moved to Eastchurch for a short while. The ground crew and equipment were transported in a couple of splendid aircraft - I think possibly a 'Bombay' together with another equally large and impressive machine.

Ground crew to whom I can put a name were: Flight Sergeant Dennard, in charge of 'A' Flight personnel, and known as 'Nodder' from his involuntary habit. He was a most able and experienced NCO and kept us all in order. Corporal Rich was our immediate superior, again an able and experienced NCO. My daily companions included C.D. 'Dickie' Bird, from

Don't forget the Erk's Sir!

Witham, Essex; George Henderson, from Reigate, Surrey, with an Aerial square-four motorcycle; Puttick, with a Norton motorcycle; J. 'Sandy' Sanderson, from Lockwood. Huddersfield, and G.S. 'Screwdriver' Tynan-Blunden, also known as 'Senora'.

Odd memories remain; 'Digging for Victory' - our vegetable patch near the dispersal hut; WAAFs playing hockey on the airfield; hot suppers from a huge Thermos flask in the dispersal hut, and frequent visits to the Chequers and the Black Horse in Fowlmere. Altogether, those few months were one of the best times of my life, and so very different from anything that had gone before.

I left Duxford / Fowlmere on 24th August 1940, when things were really hotting up. I returned three times to Fowlmere during the next twelve months, as I had the opportunity when visiting my parents in Cambridge. I saw Fowlmere or what remained of it once again not long after the war, but never since then.

Arthur 'Dave' Davis, a Londoner from Stratford had volunteered for the RAF in 1938 and was trained as an engine fitter, he along with Yorkshireman Burt 'Joe' Crawshaw had joined No. 222 Squadron at Duxford in March 1940. The squadron was at that stage equipped with Bristol Blenheims, but very soon afterwards was given notice that they would be converting to Spitfire fighters. The squadron was bloodied during the evacuation at Dunkirk and was posted to Kirton-in- Lindsey, Lincolnshire. During late August, the squadron was ordered south to partake in the Battle of Britain. Joe Crawshaw recalls:

> We had received orders to prepare quickly to go south to Hornchurch in Essex. Dave and I bundled all our belongings into my car. I had just purchased an Austin Seven motor car and was told that if I wished to take the car to Hornchurch, it

65

Don't forget the Erk's Sir!

would have to be resprayed in camouflage colours; this I did. We then began to travel in convoy, but it was so long-winded that we decided to part and go down on our own. We didn't go straight to Hornchurch, we went to Dave's home in the East End; he had recently married. I went and stayed with some friends in Welling, Kent. We eventually arrived at Hornchurch the next evening at around 5 pm.

Dave Davis continues:

> The first thing they gave us when we arrived were tin helmets 'Battle Bowlers'; I thought, well it looks like things are going to be interesting here. The squadron was pretty quite the first day, doing circuits and bumps and we settled into the scheme of things. Then in one foul swoop it really started; we were called to 15 minutes readiness. I sat in the cockpit ready to start up the aircraft, while Joe stood ready to press the electric trolley button as soon as the scramble was ordered. When this happened, Joe would help the pilot on with his parachute and strap him in; by then I would be out of the cockpit.

John Gill who was an airframe rigger, remembers his arrival at North Weald to take up his posting with No. 56 Squadron in August. The airfield had suffered an enemy raid two days previous and his introduction to the aerodrome was somewhat unusual:

> On Sunday morning I was walking through one of the hangars and I saw three airmen in blue overalls working on a Hurricane and one of them called me over and said 'have you seen a battery charger about? I said 'sorry chum I haven't', I then went to walk away and he said 'wait a minute' and beckoned me over. He then said to me 'how long have you been on this station' I told him I had

66

arrived on the Friday, just after the bombing. He then said 'In that case you won't know me, let me introduce myself, I'm the station commander and my name is Victor Beamish. I said   I'm sorry sir, I had no idea who you were'. 'That's quite alright' he said, 'be a good fellow and go at the double and try and find me a battery charger,' which I did very pronto.

These stories are just a few of the hundreds that could be told of the ground crew who worked tirelessly through those summer months of 1940 and provided the tools for our pilots to be able to engage the enemy and turn him back day after day. They should be remembered just as much as the aircrew, for without them, Fighter Command could not have functioned.

CHAPTER 5
'Hellfire Corner'

With the Germans now in full control of the coastal areas along the French side of the Channel and the moving up of Luftwaffe Air Groups occupying captured French airfields, the plans for the next phase of bringing Britain to the surrender table or invasion was put into action. In Britain, Prime Minister Churchill urged aggressively that Britain should fight on alone against Hitler and his Nazi aggression and that the British would never surrender.

The Luftwaffe Groups who were given the task of preparing the way for invasion with attacks against targets ranging from the south coast of England up to north east of England were Luftflotte 2 situated in northern France and Belgium and commanded by Generalfeldmarschall Albert Kesselring, Luftflotte 3 were based in central France, commanded by Generalfeldmarschall Hugo Sperrle and attacking the Midlands and northern Britain from across the North Sea would be Luftflotte 5, based in occupied Norway under the leadership of Generalleutnant Hans-Jurgen Stumpf.

The first phase of the attack to be undertaken was bombing of Britain's merchant naval convoys that sailed along the Channel and Thames Estuary carrying the much needed supplies from her Commonwealth Dominions and from the United States of America. Channel ports and installations would be targeted and in doing so, it was hoped the Royal Air Force would be lured into the air and destroyed.

Flight Lieutenant Roger Morewood's squadron No. 248 had been given the unenviable role of reconnaissance gathering from across the other side of the North Sea from Netherlands up to Norway and recalls their role during that summer.

> We were then given our new role as fighter reconnaissance, with operations over Norway to report any enemy shipping that was there, and we could also beat them up if the opportunity did arise. The main

object was to get back with the information and not get shot down. You had to keep your eyes open for enemy fighters nearly the whole trip. This was the squadrons main role right throughout the summer, patrolling from the Dutch coast covering up to the north of Norway; this was a six hour endurance and this was more or less the limit, if you had opened the throttle right up, you would have never got back. We did lose a hell of a lot of crews on these operations, because they weren't all that experienced. We did do night flying; our motto was 'Only bats and bloody fools fly at night.'

During the summer, up in the Shetlands it never really got dark. We weren't using any airborne radar at this stage, so all our navigation was all dead reckoning by our navigator, he would tell us 'you should be seeing the coast in half hour or whatever.' Sometimes coming back you would get hallucinations, 'there's the coast over there,' and 'can't you see it? But it would be a cloud or something else.

During the first week of July, the Luftwaffe sent out small formations of bombers and reconnaissance aircraft to probe and assess the situation before sending in a larger assault against the designated targets. A formation of twenty Dorniers attacked the naval base at Portland in Dorset on 4th July and lost one aircraft in the process, shot down by a Spitfire. No. 54 Squadron was engaged in combat with 12 Messerschmitt 109s off the coast of Deal on 9th July, the 109s had been escorting a German Red Cross seaplane, a Heinkel He59. The Heinkel was damaged during the combat and forced to beach itself at Deal, where the crew were captured and put under guard. It was later suggested that the seaplane had been used by the Germans for reconnaissance and they hoped that this would not be detected. Alan Deere was leading 'A' Flight, 54 Squadron, responsible for bringing down the German Red Cross seaplane and his report of the incident details the following:

> 'A' Flight was on patrol over Deal at 6,000 feet, when I sighted a silver seaplane approaching Deal at 100 feet. Four Messerschmitt 109s were flying above and in front, so I ordered Yellow Leader to attack the seaplane with his section, I led my section towards the escorting fighters; but in doing so I saw another 12 109s flying in loose formation close to the water.
>
> I ordered my section into line astern, but apparently my order was not received as the pilots broke away to engage the enemy. I attacked the tail-end aircraft of the original four from above and behind. It dived straight into the sea after I had given it two bursts of fire. I then pulled up climbing for height and reported to home station that the seaplane had landed in the water, ten miles east of Deal. I then dived down to attack the seaplane, but I saw a Messerschmitt endeavouring to position itself on my tail, I turned towards him and opened fire at about 1,000 yards head-on. He was also firing and I could hear his bullets striking my aircraft.
>
> We both held our fire and apparently my propeller hit some part of his fuselage as he passed overhead, as two of my propeller blades were bent right back and my hood had been pushed in. The engine vibrated tremendously and then stopped dead; smoke then began to belch out. I

was heading inland at the time of the collision and carried on for an open field to land in. Flames suddenly appeared at 1,000 feet and I was unable to see ahead, I crash-landed in a field and managed to break open my canopy and get out, although my hands were cut and bruised from efforts to get the canopy free.

Following this incident it was decided by the British Government that no German aircraft would be immune, even those flying the Red Cross; the Air Ministry forwarded the following communiqué to all fighter groups: A.M. No. 1254

It has come to the notice of His Majesty's Government in the United Kingdom, that enemy aircraft bearing civil markings and marked with the Red Cross have recently flown over British ships at sea and in the vicinity of the British coast; and that they are being employed for purposes which His Majesty's Government cannot regard as being consistent with the privileges generally accorded to the Red Cross. His Majesty's Government desire to accord to ambulance aircraft reasonable facilities for the transportation of the sick and wounded, in accordance with the Red Cross Convention, and aircraft engaged in the direct evacuation of sick and wounded will be respected, provided that they comply with the relevant provisions of the convention. His Majesty's Government are unable however, to grant immunity to such aircraft flying over areas in which operations are in progress on land and sea, or approaching British or Allied territory, or territory in British occupation, or British or Allied ships. Ambulance aircraft which do not comply with the above requirements will do so at their own risk and peril.

The communiqué literally pronounced open season on shooting down any German Red Cross aircraft entering over the Channel. Suddenly they ceased to appear.

Hellfire Corner

These sought of small incursions over to England carried on and it was not until the 10th July that the first serious raid against British shipping commenced. Records state that officially the Battle of Britain started on this day.

The weather that day was not ideal, far from it, with rain and showers over most of the south-east of England and over the Channel. During the morning the Luftwaffe sent up their regular reconnaissance sorties. One German aircraft picked up a convoy at North Foreland and immediately radioed the information back to his base. No. 74 Squadron were on patrol and flew into investigate and found the Dornier bomber with an escort of 20 Messerschmitt fighters protecting the aircraft. The six Spitfires went into the attack at 11.00 am though outnumbered and damaged the Dornier which crash-landed back in France; two Spitfires were damaged in the engagement, but were able to carrying out force-landings at Manston and Hornchurch, both pilots being uninjured. No. 610 Squadron was involved in combat with Messerschmitt fighters over Dover Harbour around the same time, when the enemy formation of 12 swept in at low level. Only one Spitfire was badly damaged, but was successfully force-landed at nearby Hawkinge aerodrome by Flight Lieutenant Andrew Smith.

It was not until early afternoon that the Germans launched an attack against a convoy (code-named 'Bread') sailing close to Dover. Just after 1.30 pm, the coastal radar at Dover began to pick large plots of aircraft formating over Cap Gris Nez in the Calais area. The information was relayed to Fighter Command Headquarters and quickly passed on to 11 Group. They immediately ordered the scramble of five squadrons to fly to the area under threat. The first on the scene over Dover were six Hurricanes of No. 32 Squadron from Biggin Hill, no sooner had they arrived over the convoy when they sighted a formation of 24-Dornier 17s with an escort of 40 mixed fighters, Messerschmitt 109s and 110s flying at various heights above the bombers. Soon after, other RAF squadrons arrived and combat entailed.

Hellfire Corner

Because of the cloudy weather that day it was increasingly difficult for the British fighters chasing the German bombers, who flew in and out of cloud to avoid detection. The other RAF squadrons who were involved in the engagement were No. 54 and 74 Squadrons from Hornchurch, 56 from North Weald, 64 based at Kenley and 111 flying from Croydon. The fighting over Dover was over in several minutes as the German formation headed back towards France. The final outcome of this engagement was the loss of one RAF Pilot, Flying Officer Higgs of 111 Squadron, who collided with a Dornier bomber of 3/KG2 whilst trying to shake off an attack by a Messerschmitt Bf109 piloted by Oberleutnant Oseau of 3/JG51. His Hurricane's wing was torn off in the collision and Higgs was forced to bale out, unfortunately his parachute failed and he was killed. In return the Germans lost eight aircraft destroyed. Only one ship was sunk.

The raids along the south-coast had not only been the Germans only incursions that day. Luftwaffe raids against Falmouth in the south-west and Swansea in South Wales, with bombing of merchant shipping, factories and railways. In all, 30 civilians had lost their lives with many more injured. So ended the first day of the battle.

For the next four days, the Luftwaffe sent raids against convoys and coastal targets. Portland and Dover again came under attack on 11th, while convoys off Oxfordness, Suffolk and North Foreland off the Kent coast were subject to bombing on 12th July, luckily the weather was quite unpredictable with cloud and thunderstorms appearing during the morning, which kept Luftwaffe raids to a minimum.

'Taffy' Higginson was patrolling as part of Blue Section, 56 Squadron at 10,000 feet over a convoy 10 miles east of Harwich at 2.15 pm on 15th July, when he sighted a formation of 12 Dorniers heading towards the ships: He reported later:

Hellfire Corner

I was flying as number three as part of blue section when I suddenly saw enemy aircraft diving out of the clouds to bomb the convoy. I broke formation and fired a preliminary burst from the beam, to try to distract the enemy aircraft intent on bombing the ships below. Most of the enemy broke away except for two or three. The leader of which dropped a bomb directly on a big ship which burst into flames. Two enemy aircraft then broke away to the right in line astern. I got on to the tail of the last one and opened fire at about 300 yards with a quarter attack, which must have put his rear gunner out of action. The enemy aircraft then adopted an echelon right formation to give the other aircraft's gunner a chance to get at me. I closed into range again and opened fire at 300 yards from astern. Both enemy aircraft then dived to sea level and I closed in to about 100 yards firing continuously. The enemy aircraft then lurched and dived straight into the sea. I was fired at by the rear gunners of both machines but luckily was not hit. The rest of the enemy jettisoned their bombs and turned eastward. They had no fighter escort.

On 16th July, Adolf Hitler issued plans drawn up by himself and other high ranking Nazis to undertake an invasion of Britain. The order titled Directive No.16 codenamed 'Operation Sealion' (Seelöwe) called for preparations by commanders of the Army, Navy and Luftwaffe to go ahead to provide the right conditions to launch an amphibious assault and allow full air support without any resistance from the Royal Air Force.

Hellfire Corner

Operation Sealion (Seelöwe)
Directive No.16

Concerning preparations for an amphibious operation against England.

Since Britain still shows no sign of willingness to come to an agreement in spite of her hopeless military situation, I have decided to prepare, and if necessary, carry out an amphibious operation against England.

The purpose of this operation will be to eliminate the English mother country as a base for continuation of the war against Germany and if it should become necessary, to occupy the entire island.

To this end I order as follows:-

1.   The amphibious operation must be carried out as a surprise crossing on a broad front extending approximately from Ramsgate to the region of the Isle of Wight, with Luftwaffe elements assuming the role of artillery and naval units assuming the role of engineers. Each individual branch of the Wehrmacht will examine from its own viewpoint whether it appears practicable to carry out subsidiary operations, for example, to occupy the Isle of Wight or Cornwall County, prior to the general crossing and will report its findings to me. I reserve the decision to myself.

2   These preparations will include the creation of conditions which will make a landing in England possibly;

a)   The English Air Force must be so far neutralised both actually and in morale, that it will offer no appreciable resistance to the German crossing operation.

 b)   Lanes must be cleared of mines.

c)   Both outlets of the Straits of Dover and the west entrance to the English Channel in a line approximately from Alderney to Portland must be sealed off by a dense belt of mines.

d) The coastal areas must be commanded and covered by the fire of heavy coastal artillery.

e)   It is desirable that all British naval forces should be tied down in action, both in the North Sea and in the Mediterranean – hereby the Italians – shortly before the crossings; efforts must be made now already by means of air and torpedo attacks to weaken as far as possible the British naval forces presently in these waters.

3.   Organisation of Command and Preparations.

Under my command and in accordance with my general directives, the commanders-in-chief of the three branches of the Wehrmacht will direct the operations of their forces employed in the operation, from 1st August on, the operations staff of the commanders-in-chief of the army, the navy, and the Luftwaffe must be within the area with a maximum radius of 30 miles from my headquarters at Ziegenberg. To me it appears advisable for the most vital elements of the operation staffs of the commanders-in-chief of the army and the navy to occupy mutual premises in Glessen. The commander-in-chief of the army will thus have to establish an army group headquarters to conduct the operations of the landing armies.

The operation will be given the designation 'Sealion' (Seelöwe). During preparations and in the execution of the operation, the mission of the three branches of the Wehrmacht will be as follows:

a)   Army. Preparation of plans of operations and of a crossing plan initially for all units to be shipped in the first wave. The units accompanying the first wave will remain under army control (under the individual landing groupments) until it is possible to subdivide their mission into responsibility for (1) support and protection for the ground forces. (2) protection of the ports of debarkation. (3) protection for the air bases to be occupied. The army will also allocate shipping space to the individual landing groupments and will define the points of embarkation and debarkation in agreement with the navy.

b)   Navy. Procurement and assemble of the required shipping space at the points of embarkation designated by the army and in accordance with nautical requirements. As far as possible use will be made of ships from defeated hostile countries. The necessary naval advisory staff, escort ships and other protective naval units will be provided by the navy at each crossing area. In addition to the protection afforded by the air units employed, naval forces will protect the flanks of the entire movement across the Channel. Orders will be issued regulating the chain of command during the actual crossing.

Another mission of the navy is to direct the uniform disposition of coastal artillery, namely, of all naval and army batteries which can be used against naval targets and to generally organise the control of fire. The largest possible number of the heaviest artillery units will be so placed that they can be brought into effective action as speedily as possible to protect the flanks of the movements against hostile naval attack. For this purpose all railway artillery, reinforced by all available captured guns but minus the K-5 and K-12 batteries earmarked for counter battery fire against shore based hostile artillery in England, will be withdrawn from present positions and emplaced on railway turntable mounts.

In addition to the above, all platform guns of the heaviest types will be so emplaced under concrete protection opposite the Straits of Dover that they will be proof against even the heaviest air attacks. They will be so sited that they will command the Straits under all circumstances as far as their range permit. The technical work involved will be carried out by organisation Todt.

c)   Luftwaffe. The mission of the Luftwaffe will be to prevent interference by hostile air forces. In addition air power will be employed to neutralise coastal fortifications which could deliver fire in the landing areas, to break the initial resistance offered by the hostile ground forces, and to destroy reserves during their forward movement. These missions will require extremely close contact between the individual air units and the landing forces of the army.

It will also be important for air units to destroy roads which could be used by the enemy to move forward reserves, and to attack naval units approaching the areas of operations whilst still far distant from the crossing routes.

Hellfire Corner

I request recommendations on the use of paratrooper and glider and other airborne forces. The question must be examined together with the army whether it would be wise to withhold paratrooper and other airborne forces during the initial stages as a reserve force which could be moved quickly to critical areas in the event of an emergency. The Wehrmacht chief signal officer will ensure that all necessary preparations are made to establish communications between France and England. Preparations will be made in co-operation with the navy to lay what is still available of the 48 miles of marine cable taken up from the East Prussian canal.

4) Preparations to ensure the necessary communications between France and English mainland will be handled by the chief of the armed forces signals.

5) I request the commanders-in-chief to submit to me as early as possible.

a) The measures planned by the navy and the Luftwaffe to create the conditions necessary for the Channel crossing operation.

b) Details on the disposition of the coastal artillery batteries (Navy)

c) A survey of the shipping to be employed and of the methods of concentration and equipment. All civilian agencies participate? (Navy)

d) Plans for the organisation of air defence in the areas of concentration for troops and for equipment to be used in the crossing operation (Luftwaffe).

e) Channel crossing schedule and plan of operation of the army, and organisation and equipment of the first attack wave.

f) Organisation and action plan by the navy and the Luftwaffe for the defence of the crossing movement itself for reconnaissance and for support during the landing.

g) Recommendations concerning the commitment of paratrooper and other airborne forces and concerning the commander forces after an adequately large area has been brought under control in England (Luftwaffe).

h)   Recommendations for the location of headquarters for the command   echelons of the commander-in-chief of the army and the commander-in-chief of the navy.
i)   Comments by the army, the navy and the Luftwaffe as to weather and what partial operations are considered practicable prior to the general amphibious operation.
k)   Recommendations by the army and navy concerning the chain of command during the crossing while seaborne.

Signed
Adolf Hitler

As Fighter Command began to make up the losses of casualties suffered during the fighting in France and Dunkirk in late May and June, many new pilots were now arriving at their new squadrons having completed their training at the Operational Training Units. One such newcomer was Sergeant Len Davies aged 19:

> I joined 151 Squadron at North Weald on 17th July 1940 and the commanding officer at that time was a chap named Wing Commander Edward Donaldson; he was quite an experienced pilot and had already shot down a number of aircraft over France during May.   I remember him coming over to the flight to give us a talk about our role and what to expect from the Germans. As far as tactics; at the OTU's it was basically familiarisation on the aeroplane, we didn't get much information and I had only fired my guns once at a target. From July till things really hotted up in August it was learning on the job so to speak, a bit of formation flying and verbal tuition about flying line astern. No.151 took a hell of a pasting because those lad's who were the same age as

myself, 18 and 19 didn't have the experience and most of them didn't see what hit them. It was experience you needed and we weren't getting it, we were still learning how to fly the aeroplane and feel comfortable with it. You needed to be able to concentrate entirely outside.

Geoffrey Page, a Hurricane pilot serving with No. 56 Squadron operating from North Weald recalls one of his early actions against the Luftwaffe:

One of our early experiences was when a flotilla, if that's the right naval expression for small torpedo boats, had gone out to attack their German equivalent off Calais or Dunkirk and two British destroyers also went out. Then the Germans retaliated by sending out a large force of Stuka dive-bombers to bomb the British vessels with a fighter escort. This was quite fun because when the Stuka's peeled off to attack the destroyers, we peeled off after them very much like a pack of cards, one German, one Hurricane, one German, one Hurricane and I think we got about six Stuka's. Don't forget once the Stuka's pulled out of their dive at sea-level, they then had to fly back to France, virtually ten feet above the waves and by throttling back our engines, we could get in behind the Stuka and there was the poor rear gunner with his single pop gun to defend his aeroplane against our eight machine guns. They were a pretty easy target. We were able to knock them off just like skittles.

Hellfire Corner

Flight Lieutenant Alan Deere flying with 54 Squadron based at Hornchurch remembers the early stages of the battle:

> The Battle of Britain was a gradual build-up. In July, we were doing convoy patrols again, because at that time the Germans had occupied the Channel coast and the convoys had to be protected. We had the odd engagements; I had one engagement and managed to shoot down one of the Huns. As the tempo built up, we were doing three to four sorties a day, and mostly getting into combat.
>
> The Germans were getting more and more aggressive as they built up their forces on the other side of the Channel. Their penetration at the time was only twenty to thirty miles inland, but their intention was to harass and bomb the convoys and also get our squadrons up and knock us out. Fortunately Dowding and Keith Park realised this was probably their aim and therefore the number of squadrons committed to battle at any one time was fairly restricted, so we always had a reserve.

Sergeant Len Davies No. 151 Squadron:

> We use to operate from Rochford near Southend, fly down there at 4 o'clock in the morning. Because we were very close to the Thames Estuary, we would wait for the call to scramble. Most of our initial work was patrolling convoys at the beginning of the battle, which kept us quite busy. The first experience I had

was against a formation of Stuka dive-bombers who were attacking on the coast. I and another chap saw three of these aircraft heading back out to sea, quite low at about 1,000 feet. They flew into cloud and we followed them; I had my first experience of close formation flying using the blind flying instruments instead of using your instincts. When we came out of the cloud, we could see them in the distance, but we never got close enough to them. I must recall that the adrenalin was really going, not fear.

Flight Lieutenant Peter Brothers was leading 'B' Flight of 32 Squadron during the late afternoon of 20th July and was given instructions from his ground controller that a German formation was nearing Folkestone. Little did he know that the next few minutes would be so harrowing?

I was leading Blue Section that day, when I saw a number of enemy bombers start to attack a convoy off Folkestone. There was about 30 Messerschmitt 109s above on guard, so I climbed to attack them while Red and Green Sections went for the bombers. I attacked one Messerschmitt and set him on fire. As I got on the tail of a second, two 109s in line astern attacked me head on. A third was on my tail and a fourth was firing a full deflection shot at me from my right. I attacked the first head on and as they passed over my head, I turned steeply to the right and fired at the one on my right. Afterwards I tried to get on to the tail of the one behind me, unfortunately I lost him and as I finished all but about 20 rounds of my ammunition, I decided to circle round and try and get my section together. As I could neither find nor get in touch with them, I landed to refuel and re-arm.

Pilot Officer George 'Ben' Bennions No. 41 Squadron:

> The first time I shot anything down was on 28th July, which was confirmed by Pilot Officer Wally Wallens, when I claimed a Messerschmitt 109 at 2.30 pm at 20,000 feet over Dover, the following day I claimed another, but I had to make a forced landing at Manston due to my Spitfire being badly damaged by enemy gunfire.

Percy Morfill was flying with 501 Squadron on 29th July and relates the sequence of events that he was engaged in:

> The enemy aircraft were seen diving out of the sun, their target being Dover Harbour. The squadron was flying south, south east, having just turned around from the opposite course (flying into sun). Due to our position, it was necessary to continue on a southerly course and turn right of the harbour. This was to avoid the anti-aircraft fire over the harbour itself. 501 were detailed for destruction of the bombers. I attacked one Junkers Ju87 and on closing to 250 yards range, gave the enemy a good burst. Tracer appeared to strike the enemy aircraft. The aircraft then used violent evasive tactics, turns to both left and right. I overshot him and fired on a second Ju87. Owing to the close range obtained, I considered that both of

these enemy machines were damaged. On breaking away from the second bomber, a 109 was seen to be firing at me from rear quarter. I immediately turned sharp right and after more than a couple of turns, I found the enemy aircraft in front at a range of approximately 100 yards. I fired using almost full deflection as smoke began to belch from his engine. The pilot baled out and after a couple of seconds, his machine dived into the sea. Fortunately for the pilot his parachute had opened.

By the end of July, the Luftwaffe's attempts at causing heavy losses amongst the merchant shipping along the Channel had been very minimal. They had managed to sink 18 steamers and four Royal Navy destroyers; but in return had lost 270 aircraft against the RAF in combat and the anti-aircraft defences on land and sea. Fighter Command losses stood at 145.

Clashes continued through the early days of August, while weather conditions remained unsettled and halted any major attacks. German weather intelligence predicted that a high pressure system would be moving up from South Atlantic giving a break of ideal weather by the second week.

On 8th August, a vital British convoy code-named 'Peewit' was scheduled to pass along the Channel heading out into the Atlantic. The 20-ship convoy had set sail the previous night along the Thames Estuary, but its progress had been picked up by German radar at Wissant on the northern coast of France. During the early morning the convoy was attacked by German motor torpedo boats (E-boats) and three of the convoy were sunk.

At approximately 9.00 am, radar picked up a formation of Luftwaffe aircraft as they headed in towards the convoy approaching from the Cherbourg area. This formation consisted of Junkers Ju87s from Fliegerkorps VIII and

Hellfire Corner

Messerschmitt 109S of JG27. The information was relayed to controllers at 10 and 11 Group who in turn sent off five squadrons to intercept the dive-bombers and their escorts before reaching the convoy. The German force was broken up and was forced to retreat.

The Germans sent out another force of Ju87s in an attempt to try and sink the convoy at 12.45 pm, by which time the merchantmen were steaming just off the Isle of Wight. Again the Stukas were met by RAF fighters and were severely punished. Squadron Leader George Darley was commanding officer of No. 609 'West Riding' Squadron based at Warmwell; his squadron was scrambled and detailed to attack the raiders over the Isle of Wight. In his report for that day he states:

> B Flight was ordered to patrol 'Peewit' at 10,000 feet. After taking off I climbed from 1 – 4000 feet, and after climbing again to 7,000 feet I could not see the objective owing to a layer of cloud below. I informed the controller and went below cloud to 3,500 feet north of the convoy.
>
> I then saw a balloon coming down in flames and turned towards the convoy. I observed an enemy aircraft diving on the convoy and as I approached five Messerschmitt 110s had just finished a dive and were climbing up below me and in the opposite direction.
>
> I gave the order to attack independently and turned right about and dived down on the 110s and after that I lost contact with the remainder of my flight. I was not in a good position for the 110s, so I climbed up again and saw one of the enemy a mile ahead, heading due south. I then flew in and out of cloud and then dived down and

opened fire in a one and half second burst at 250 yards, then another at 75 yards. As I turned away, I saw the enemy machine bank steeply to port, then I broke away to the right and turned back to see the enemy aircraft hit the sea.

My attack was a quarter attack, aiming at the starboard engine and pilot's cabin. Return fire at first from the rear gunner. I then circled the neighbourhood and made a full defection attack on a 110 at 200 yards with no apparent result; and also did a head-on attack on a Junkers Ju87 at 200 yards, again with no result. Also attacked another Ju87 coming straight on at 300 feet above. Fired a short burst; but no results. I observed a single-seat fighter pursued by another. The target burst into flames, did a half roll and went straight into the sea. I saw a parachute coming down into the sea about 10 miles south of the convoy. Most of the action was spent 5-10 miles south of the convoy, where there was a clear patch of sky. As I could no longer see any more aircraft in my area, I returned to base.

The German losses amongst the Stukas that day were very high and in all nine were lost; in addition nine escorting Messerschmitt 109s were also shot down. The RAF faired little better having suffered the loss of 17 aircraft destroyed which included a Blenheim and the loss of 19 aircrew killed in total that day. The protection of the convoy had been costly to both sides.

The convoy 'Peewit' sailed on having suffered a further four ships sunk, six badly damaged along with another six armed rescue vessels. This day had witnessed the largest attempt by the Luftwaffe to sink a convoy during this period of the battle. There was never to be such large scale attempts again after this.

CHAPTER 6

Airfields and Radar come under attack

During the second week of August, a change of tactics was initiated by the Luftwaffe High Command and orders were given to attack the Royal Air Force Fighter Stations and knock out the Radio Direction Finding Stations (Radar) situated along the Channel coast.

The task of knocking out the vital aerodromes in the south-east would then open up the opportunity to not only destroy the RAF Fighters in the air, but cripple them on the ground. Once this was done, the invasion could start in earnest.

The first main attack by the Luftwaffe was scheduled for Monday 12th August, which involved attacking the coastal radar chain at Pevensey, Dover, Rye and Dunkirk. Three of the stations were hit, but damage was minimal and was soon back in operation. One bombing raid by Junker Ju88s of KG51 hit the radar at Ventnor on the Isle of Wight later that day and was put out of action for several weeks.

Alan Deere, now a seasoned fighter pilot after fighting and surviving the battles over Dunkirk, remembered the first raids:

> Eventually of course, the Germans came over and their targets were the coastal airfields such as Manston, Hawkinge and Tangmere. Then the real fighting started in that we were not only coping with fighter escorts, but with bombers as well. Gradually they moved their penetration further and further until they were bombing the airfields that lined the outskirts of London, where all the sector controls were based.

During the afternoon of the 12th, the first raids against RAF airfields in Kent were undertaken, Manston was first, attacked at 12.45 pm, followed by Lympne and Hawkinge. The damage caused was heavy, but the airfields were soon patched up and remained operational.

Douglas Grice of No. 32 Squadron had been in action that day and was heading back to his forward base at Hawkinge on the Kent coast, when he received a radio transmission from his controller on the ground:

> I suddenly heard over my R/T; 'don't land at Hawkinge the airfield has been bombed.' So being very curious I flew back to Hawkinge and there were considerable signs of damage and the airfield seemed to have mole hills on it. I thought this looks interesting, I could see a path between the mole hills, and so I landed and taxied between them to where earlier I had taken off from. The flight sergeant came over and said 'I think you better take-off again very quickly sir,' so I said 'Why? He said 'you see all those mole hills, they're unexploded bombs,' How innocent we were, I had not realised this of course, so I took his advice and weaved my way through the mole hills and took off rather smartly and flew back to Biggin Hill

No. 65 Squadron had been caught on the ground during the attack on Manston by Messerschmitt Bf110s and Junkers Ju88s, fortunately most of the pilots had managed to get their Spitfires airborne, while bombs rained down on the aerodrome. Dave Glaser, a young pilot officer aged 19 years recalls the desperate effort to avoid the raid:

> The Germans had come in unseen at low-level and the bombs were dropping all over the place. Everybody just opened up their throttles and went hell for leather to

get their aircraft off the ground. A bomb
exploded just behind Pilot Officer Wigg's
aeroplane, which stopped his propeller.
Nobody had ever seen Wigg run for a
scramble, but they reported that he ran
like blazes for cover into a hedgerow.
Dick Kilner, who was a sergeant pilot, he
managed to get out of his aircraft. He had
been waiting to have his oxygen bottle
changed, when his ground crew suddenly
disappeared from view; so he bolted for
the nearest shelter where he found them.
Apart from that everybody managed to
get off safely.

Norman Hayes was a flying officer pilot with Bristol
Blenheim 600 Squadron and he was also on the ground at
Manston, when it was attacked:

Manston was heavily bombed and I can
remember I was just off the airfield during
the first raid. The Germans had been
raiding shipping in the Channel for some
weeks and on this occasion I was walking
with 'Dicky' Haine when suddenly we
heard the sound of lots of aeroplanes, but
we didn't take too much notice as we had
heard aircraft engines many times before,
but this time it seemed to be getting closer
and closer, as we looked up there were
Messerschmitt 110s diving on the airfield.
They dropped something like one
hundred bombs which all fell within the
perimeter of the aerodrome, but not one
person was killed. We had been very
lucky.

No.56 Squadron had been scrambled late afternoon from
North Weald to intercept raiders. Just off the coast off

Airfields and Radar come under attack

Margate they encountered a formation of Dorniers of KG2 and went into the attack. Geoffrey Page recalls the event that would change his life forever:

> It was about five o'clock in the evening and we were all sitting around having tea on the grass alongside a tent, within the tent was a field telephone with a handle, which if you wound the handle the bell rang; it was connected to the sector operations. They rang through about this time and said that there was an attack coming in. Our squadron by this time had been losing quite a few people; we were supposed to muster twelve aircraft for the attack on the enemy, but in fact we only had ten. So the ten of us took off and the usual procedure of the controller said 'there are ninety Bandit's approaching from the south,' which were at about 15,000 feet. As we climbed up, we could see a swarm of what looked like insects beginning to take shape; it was a large formation of Dornier 17 bombers escorted by their 109 fighters.
>
> I was in the leading section of three and the one nearest the German bombers and on the right hand side, I could see some tracer ammunition coming from the whole formation, they had singled me out as the target. They probably had a radio control officer who had singled me out to shoot at. Suddenly all these things that looked lethal electric light bulbs came flashing by and then suddenly I heard an enormous bang and then the whole aircraft just exploded.
>
> The scientists reckon that the temperature goes up from a cool room

91

temperature at 15,000 feet to 3,000 degrees centigrade in ten seconds; so if you don't get out in the first few seconds; you are not going to get out. It was then that the excellent RAF training came to my rescue, when I instinctively carried out the drill for releasing the harness that strapped me to my seat, I then slid the hood back, turned the aircraft on to its back and kicked the flying control column, so the aircraft pointed its nose up and I was shot out of the cockpit like a cork out of a toy gun.

Stupidly I had not been wearing any gloves, later on it became mandatory to wear gloves; my hands got a terrible burning as did my face as well. My mouth and nose were saved by my oxygen mask. I then found myself tumbling head over heels in space, I remember seeing my right arm extended, I looked at it and my brain ordered it to bring it in and pull the metal ring on the ripcord of my parachute. This was agony because trying to pull the metal ring with a badly burned hand was like feeling an electric shock. I didn't have a choice, it was either pull it or the parachute wouldn't open. It opened and I found myself floating down; my first instinct was to look up and see if the parachute was on fire, but fortunately it wasn't and then I took stock of the situation and I noticed that a funny thing had happened. My left shoe and trousers had been blown off completely by the explosion; I was almost naked from the waist down and my legs were slightly burned. I could still hear the fight going on around me, because when you're on a parachute there was no engine noise, it's surprising how sound travels.

It took me about ten minutes to float down into the water and then there were various other problems I had to contend with. Firstly, when I hit the water I had to get rid of the parachute, you do this by turning a metal release buckle which is just over your stomach, through 90- degrees, then give it a hard thump, then all of the parachute harness breaks away. But my hands were so badly burned that it was difficult to do this; so I found myself in the water connected to the chute and it was all over me and I was more or less covered by all the chords. I knew if I didn't get away from the parachute quickly it would get waterlogged and sink and take me with it. Out of desperation I managed to painfully. I thought the next thing now is to blow up my life saving jacket which had a little tube just below ones left shoulder; I tried blowing it up, but only small bubbles appeared in the water as the jacket had been burned through.

My face was beginning to swell up from the burns by then and I couldn't get my helmet off, the leather strap had been so badly seared that I just couldn't undo it. I began to swim off, my eyesight was not beginning to fail, but my swollen eyelids were beginning to close up and the distant view of England which I could see a few miles away was getting more and more blurred. So I started swimming and then a happy thought came into my mind that in my jacket pocket was a brandy flask that my dear mother had given me, which I had filled with brandy, thinking on some

occasion or other there would be an
emergency and I would need it. As I was
swimming along I thought this probable
qualifies as an emergency. So on that
happy thought, I rolled on to my back
kicking my legs and that was another
painful episode trying to get the flask
from within my tunic, eventually I
managed to grasp it between my hands
and undone the cap with my teeth. I lifted
it up to take a swig of brandy and at that
moment a dirty big wave came along and
knocked it out of my wrists and the whole
lot went to the bottom of the Channel; I
was a little bit annoyed about that.

After a while I heard more than saw a
boat, there were two men in it and it was
interesting, they kept asking me questions,
by this time I had been swimming for
about half an hour and I was a bit tired
and fed up with the whole affair, so when
they said to me 'are you a Jerry' and this
and that, I'm afraid I let loose with every
rude four letter word that I could think of.
That immediately assured them that I was
an RAF officer and they then took me to
a big ship, where the captain dressed my
burns with lint and they gave me a cup of
tea. Then the Margate lifeboat came out
and took me off the Trinity life house
vessel into Margate and the hospital there;
and for the first time for over an hour or
so, I was able to laugh because on the
quayside was the Mayor of Margate
dressed in a tail suit and top hat. It was
funny after being in an air fight only an
hour or so before to see a chap in coat
tails welcoming you to Margate.

Airfields and Radar come under attack

The following day, Tuesday 13th August was to have seen a more comprehensive attack by the German Air Force. Titled by the Germans as 'Adler Tag' (Eagle Day) the raid was postponed initially during the early morning due to weather conditions and the raids did not resume until the afternoon, but weather still was poor. Dornier bombers did manage to attack RAF Eastchurch and destroy five Bristol Blenheim light-bombers, as well as damage hangars and block houses. In reality the day was a failure for the Luftwaffe, with the loss of thirty-four aircraft lost to thirteen suffered by the RAF.

Squadron Leader John Marlow Thompson was commanding officer of No. 111 Squadron home-based at Croydon, he flew on 13th August and relates how difficult it was to find and engage the enemy due to the weather conditions:

> At 5.50 am the squadron took off on a vector heading of 125 degrees and a height 12,000 feet. After 12 minutes we were told to orbit, but shortly afterwards we were ordered to patrol our forward base at Hawkinge, below cloud and look for enemy aircraft approaching from the north-east. We were then told to proceed on a vector of 340 degrees below cloud and look for German aircraft returning from the direction of the Isle of Sheppey. No enemy aircraft were observed on this course. On arrival over Eastchurch I was unable to contact the ground station by radio and owing to poor visibility, I went above the clouds. At approximately 7.10 hours a formation was observed approaching from the east about 1,000 feet below us. It was a formation in section of three astern of about 10 aircraft, but owing to the distance they could not be identified. I instructed 'A'

95

Flight leader to remain where he was, whilst I took my flight past these aircraft on the port beam to identify them.

When I identified them as Dorniers, I instructed my 'A' Flight leader to carry out a head-on attack, whilst I took my flight around to the rear. At that moment I observed another formation astern of the first one, so I carried on and executed a head-on attack on this from below. Little return fire was observed until we broke away. These head-on attacks certainly had the effect of breaking up the enemy formations. I then attacked the formation from the rear, closing within 200 yards of the right hand aeroplane. I broke away from this attack and observed another Dornier alone over Sittingbourne, flying east. I carried out a full deflection attack, closing astern to about 50 yards. Both engines started to emit clouds of white vapour, but the German pilot pulled up into the clouds. This aircraft could not possibly have flown on much more than a few miles.

On my return to base I sighted a Dornier over West Malling, which appeared out of the clouds ahead of me. I gave him a two second burst of my guns at about 400 yards range, but he too went immediately back into cloud. Owing to shortage of fuel I then returned to base and landed.

It was later confirmed that the first Dornier that Thompson had attacked was listed as belonging to 3/KG2 and had failed to return.

Colin Gray remembers the events that his squadron, No. 54 undertook on 15th and 16th August:

Airfields and Radar come under attack

On 15th and 16th we were busy again. On the 15th, I had to go up to the Ministry of Supply in London for a discussion in the morning, but the squadron went down to Manston where they were involved in intercepting a raid on nearby Lympne. Two of our pilots, Sergeants Lawrence and Klozinski were shot down and finished up in hospital. I returned from London during the afternoon and was scrambled about 6.30 pm against a raid of Dorniers escorted by the usual 109s. I used up all my ammunition against a Dornier with no positive result. Two more of our pilots were again shot down, Pilot Officer Matthews, who was unhurt and Al Deere who finished up in East Grinstead Hospital with a nasty wrist injury, but the doctors couldn't keep him there.

Leading Aircraftsman Michael Evans was stationed at Tangmere and was there on the 16th August, when it received a surprise unwelcome visit by German dive-bombers.

I was walking with a couple of mates across the main square and we looked up to see Ju87s diving down on us from out of the sun, having just released their bombs.

I knew where the nearest shelter was, just inside the double doors of the nearby barrack block. As I ran towards it, I was lifted up off my feet by the blast, the double doors opened ahead of me and I slid down the stairs into the shelter. The earth shook and shook again as the bombing continued unabated. Some

Airfields and Radar come under attack

WAAF's who had previously been showering were now clad only in their dressing gowns were also in the shelter with us. For some reason we all joined hands and started singing together until the bombing had ceased.

When we looked out the area was devastated. The top of our block was sheared off and the armoury was still burning with intermittent explosions. One shelter had been hit and dead and injured WAAFs were being brought out on stretchers. We found later that one of our squadron of fighters had failed to meet any enemy aircraft and were returning to base, when they looked down and saw their own aerodrome being bombed. Diving down from height to the Ju87s, they shot every one down.

That night, with my two friends, I was despatched to guard a crashed German aircraft in the grounds of Arundel Castle. There were crashed German aeroplanes all across the countryside. The night was memorable for several silly reasons. When we were dropped off in the dark to guard the aircraft, we were told that the bombs might still be aboard and there might be a German pilot who had parachuted and he might still be in the area and he would be armed. With my two friends, Hughes and Kennedy, we decided that it would be safer to guard the aircraft from the opposite side of the grassy bank and put ourselves between it, should a bomb go off. We took it in turn to guard the aircraft and I was on the first watch at 1.00 am, when I heard the snapping of

98

Airfields and Radar come under attack

twigs, fortunately it was only a cow, which had wandered in.

When my turn came to sleep after being relieved, I was awoken by a hard blow on my nose and I quickly defended myself thinking I was now being attacked by the German pilot. As I struggled with my attacker in the dark, I managed to get my hands around his neck. Suddenly I realised it was my friend Kennedy, who while he was asleep had accidentally flung out his arm and struck me. He had been equally convinced that I was a German. We returned to Tangmere the following morning both having faced death twice in the same day.

The following piece is a letter sent by Aircraftsman Len Swift to his mother in which he wrote following about the bombing of Tangmere on 16th August.

Dear Mother

I arrived here on time yesterday and was astounded to find that the aerodrome had been bombed to hell at dinner time on Friday, everybody is now air-raid conscious and when the alarm goes you should see them run.

I am writing this in a field outside the drome during our third raid today. All those on duty jump the boundary wire, when the alarm is given, and having seen the damage done by the raid on Friday, I am content to get outside the aerodrome as quickly as I can.

While sitting here we have heard at least a dozen bombs drop a bit too near for our liking, but far enough away to prevent our seeing any effects of it.

There is not a building on the aerodrome which does not show some effect of the bombs, and it is a miracle there were not more killed than 12 and 60 injured. Out of the 54 fellows I came here with, only one is dead, but several had

Airfields and Radar come under attack

near misses. They tell me that all the bombs were dropped within six minutes.

I have just discovered a peculiar smell like sh-t in this ditch and on investigation I have discovered I have been sitting in some, much to my disgust and my two pal's amusement.

It is now 6.00 pm Monday night and I have been on fatigues all day long clearing up some of the mess around, and have had two alarms this afternoon, but no aircraft got very near, although one machine dropped four bombs outside the drome and was immediately shot down by a Spitfire.

There has been a lot of bother over the airmen taking cover outside the drome, so we are now supposed to go to our shelters inside. As you can imagine it has upset a lot of things here, there is still no electric light on yet and the water is only on in some places. I was rather annoyed when I moved last Thursday to my present billet, because it is so far away from the cookhouse, but now I don't mind the distance now and am quite thankful to be away from the flying field.

Every hangar here bar one had a direct hit and a lot of planes on the field were disabled, when they dropped the bombs, they machine-gunned the men as they ran for shelter and did the same to one of the ambulances, you should see the huge craters made by the bombs.

If this letter seems a bit sketchy, you must remember that I am jotting things down as I think of them. Oh yes, all the bombers were brought down and none got back to tell the tale, altogether there were 28 bombs dropped.

Well Mother that's all for now and don't worry because they have done the damage now.

Your loving son
Len

Mike Hodges served as an aircraft instrument repairer and was stationed at North Weald with No. 56 Squadron. In his diary he recalled an attack on the airfield:

Airfields and Radar come under attack

In mid August things hotted up. A typical day would start at 4.30 am, when aircraft were warmed up and sometimes they would fly off to a coast drome and then come back later on. One morning I had just got back into my bed, when 257 Squadron arrived for the day. This was a rather busy day with air-raid alarms and our aircraft returning at dusk to require servicing. There were a lot of oxygen bottles for me to change.

On 16th August at lunchtime, the squadron scrambled and were all airborne in three minutes. A few minutes later over fifty German aircraft appeared out of the clouds at 15,000 feet, and we saw our fighters go into attack. Bombs dropped mainly to the south of the drome, but some buildings were damaged. We were able to watch all of this from the door of the shelter, as we were on the north side. Our aircraft returned at about 5.40 pm having got some of the attacking German's.

Avis Hearn was a WAAF Chain Home radar operator during the battle; Avis was working at the CH site at Poling on the West Sussex coast. As the German raids intensified, she recalls the day that her station came under attack:

August 18th was the day our station was hit. When we went on duty that day, the sergeant met us and said we would have to change over quickly with the other crew as they had picked up a massive formation of aircraft forming up over Calais. He asked for one of us to go over to the new R Block. We were working at that time in wooden huts which were only protected by sandbags. They had just built a new brick building with a concrete roof which was terribly thick and also bomb proof doors. I went over into that room to take over from another WAAF who was receiving plots from radar called CHL (Chain Home Low) that picked up the low flying aircraft. They could only get their plots through us because the GPO didn't have enough lines. This is how I came to be there.

When the enemy raid began, the sergeant told me to duck, which meant take cover, but I couldn't, I told him I have simply too much information coming through. If I had run or taken cover the information might have changed and if I had not got it through, Fighter Command would not have received vital changes.

While this was all going on a civilian walked in, didn't know who he was and at the time I had to work two headphone sets, one to Truleigh Hill, the other to Fighter Command at Stanmore. I got this chap to help me out by repeating the information. I was then called up by one of the operators at Truleigh and told that the enemy plot was dead overhead of us at Poling; suddenly I could hear the sound of bombs exploding.

The German aircraft were Junkers dive-bombers and as they dived down they screamed, they gave a hideous noise which was frightening. After about twenty minutes the communication line went dead. A bomb had hit the feeder lines, so we couldn't get anymore plots through to Fighter Command; we still had a telephone line so we could let them know the situation, but we were out of action. When I made my way out of the building I noticed that one of the bomb proof doors had been twisted due to a bomb blast. One of our officers had recently bought a beautiful Lagonda car, when I came out I noticed it had been hit and was a complete write-off. Another officer appeared who had red lapels on his tunic collars; I think he was in charge of the gun-site which was there to protect us. He collected the other two girls from the other hut and one which had taken cover underground and bundled us into a car and away from the site.

The station itself, there was bomb craters everywhere and it was a complete mess. A total of ninety bombs had been dropped, the receiver block had been demolished and the aerials had been blown down A few days later they then sent us a mobile radar unit and this was set up and hidden in a wood at Angmering. There were two large caravans; one was for the transmitter, the other for the receiver. We managed like that until October, which filled the gap; this is what Ventnor had to do as well. You can imagine what it was like stuck in a small caravan for eight hours at a go.

That same day, the RAF aerodrome at Kenley also was subject to a surprise attack, when at approximately 1.22 pm, a large force consisting of between thirty and fifty bombers approached their target at between 15,000 – 20, 000 feet, while a smaller force of nine Dornier 17s of 9/KG76 with fighter escort came in avoiding radar detection at a height of fifty feet. As information came in to the operations room regarding the height and path of the enemy force, Hurricane pilots of No. 111 Squadron at nearby Croydon were scrambled and ordered to patrol the line between Croydon and Kenley.

The ground-defences at Kenley had now been forewarned by the Observer Corps, who sighted the low flying German formation heading their way. One pilot of 615 Squadron, Pilot Officer Keith Lofts was just in the process of becoming airborne, when suddenly the Dornier bombers appeared over the aerodrome boundary. Lofts was confronted with the prospect of a head-on collision, which he fortunately adverted by swinging his aircraft into a sharp right turn.

The Dorniers proceeded to strafe with machine guns and drop their special time-delay bombs across the aerodrome. Three hangars were hit and set alight immediately. Another bomb hit the hospital block and a shelter where personnel had been congregated. The aerodromes defences were now pouring every anti-aircraft and machine gun into the sky to try and knock down the enemy aircraft. One of the aerodrome defences that Kenley had in its arsenal was a device called Parachute & Cable. This device was worked by an operator shooting three wire cables into the air by a line of rockets across the path of the enemy aircraft. This could be used and set to a height of 600 feet. Once the aircraft had become entangled with one or two of the cables on its wings, the parachute was opened on the cables and this would create a drag pull of one tonne. This would cause the pilot to lose control, would cause the aircraft to slow and stall, causing it to fall to the ground.

As the Dorniers swept across Kenley, Aircraftsman D. Roberts fired one of these devices into the air and caught one of the enemy bombers in the cables. It crashed into a tree and broke up, catching fire and sending debris across a large area including hitting a bungalow. As the remaining Dorniers began to make their homeward journey back towards France, they were attacked by Hurricanes of No. 111 Squadron and were harassed all the way. One bomber flown by the Hauptmann Joachim Roth, the commander of

Airfields and Radar come under attack

9/KG76 was shot down and crash-landed in a field at Leaves Green near Biggin Hill. Both he and his crew survived and became prisoners of war. Out of the nine German raiders, four were lost and two crash-landed after sustaining heavy damage during the attack.

Jim Croft was serving as a Clerk (Special Duties) in the Operations Room at Kenley and clearly recalls the day of the raid:

> I had been on duty in the Ops Room overnight and after breakfast attended at the station sick quarters at 11.15 am for some dental treatment. I had not been there long before a message came over the Tannoy system, 'Attack alarm, attack alarm'. All personnel not servicing aircraft take cover'. The broadcast came from the Ops Room when enemy aircraft were in close proximity. Our building was immediately evacuated and I joined my colleagues outside the covered slit trench which was directly behind our billets.
>
> We were enjoying a chat and a smoke outside the shelter as we had done in the past weeks, for although there was plenty of air activity, nothing much up to now had happened. However, on this day we were suddenly being attacked by machine gun and cannon fire as three Dornier aircraft, at low level flew over the rooftops of our billets. There was a mad scramble to get underground and from then on, all hell broke loose.
>
> Our trench had a near miss at one end and a few of our colleagues were partially buried. However, no serious casualties were sustained and we emerged into the daylight about 1.00 pm to survey the damage.

Airfields and Radar come under attack

The sick quarters where I had been earlier was in flames and the shelter adjacent to the building had received a direct hit, we learned later that three of our medical officers had been killed, including a well known local doctor. Of the seven hangars on the aerodrome, only one remained intact and a pall of smoke hung over the area. Strangely, although communications were severely damaged, the Operations Room had not been hit, but it was decided that the building should be abandoned and staff transferred to the 'Emergency Operations Room' which had been constructed inside a converted butchers shop in Caterham-in-the Valley, owned pre-war by Messrs Spice and Wallis.

Twenty-year old Iris Cockle had joined the Women's Auxiliary Air Force in 1939 and had been posted to Kenley and had only been there for about a week, when she underwent her baptism of fire:

I was working in the equipment section, where we were responsible for everything from aircraft parts to clothing and rations. That afternoon during a quit spell, the sergeant asked me to take over while he and a few colleagues took a break. Shortly afterwards the sound of the air-raid sirens sounded across the airfield and the next thing I saw were German aircraft hedge-hopping across Kenley; dropping their bombs and raking the area with gunfire.

I threw myself into the section's dugout to find I was the only occupant. For the next few minutes, I just sat there frozen with fear as the air raid continued about me. Then came the deafening silence after the planes had passed over, followed by the sound of a voice shouting out 'Hey Blondie, you better get out of there. There's an unexploded bomb on the roof of your dugout! It was a young airman who had stuck his head into the dugout to see if anyone was still alive.

When I came out into the light, all I could see was devastation everywhere. There were great scoops ripped into the ground that had been created by the bombs. Rubble from what were once buildings lay scattered everywhere. Vehicles lay on their sides with smoke and flames billowing from them. A German aircraft had buried itself nose down in the ground. Worst of all was the sight of comrades lying either dead or injured. Fortunately for me, what had landed on my dugout, turned out to be an empty shell case?

No. 64 Squadron who was also based at the aerodrome was already airborne having been scrambled at 12.55 pm. They were led by their commanding officer, Squadron Leader Donald MacDonell who hastily got eight airworthy Spitfires into action. He remembers the urgency of the situation:

As soon as we were all off the ground and climbing, I informed operations that 'Freema Squadron was airborne. They came back and told me to patrol over base at 20,000 feet. We missed the first low-level raid, but we were in position to engage, when twenty minutes later a larger formation of various bombers with fighter escort came in to bomb Kenley from high altitude. I gave a quick call over the R/T

Airfields and Radar come under attack

'Freema Squadron, Bandits below! 'Tally
Ho' and down we went in a wide spiral
manoeuvre, making sure that there were
no German fighters lurking above us. I
managed to latch onto a Messerschmitt
110 from astern and gave it a couple of
short bursts from my guns. It went into a
steep dive with both its engines belching
smoke.

The Messerschmitt shot down by MacDonell finally came
to earth, crash-landing on Dering Farm at Lydd. It
belonged to Stab I/ZG26 and both its crew Oberleutnant
Proske and Unteroffizier Mobius both survived and were
captured.

Also flying with 64 Squadron that day was Pilot Officer
Richard Jones, he remembers that one of his colleagues
who had not been scrambled, had been caught in an
awkward position:

I can recall that Jackie Mann was sitting
on the bog seat, when part of the lavatory
was blown away by a bomb exploding
nearby. It must have been a hell of a
shock, but fortunately he survived to fight
another day.

As the aerodromes personnel began to begin to evaluate the
damage that stood before them and help with the wounded;
it was at this time that the main enemy force arrived and
began dropping high explosive bombs from high altitude.
Fortunately, some of the German bomber force on already
seeing heavy smoke and fires burning below, decided to
turn their attention to other targets.

After the raid, bomb disposal teams were sent in to
secure and mark out those bombs which had failed to
detonate. Over one hundred bombs had been dropped over
the aerodrome of which twenty-five had failed to go off.
RAF losses on the ground that day were ten aircraft, while

human casualties consisted of nine RAF personnel killed and eight wounded. A soldier of the 12th Home Defence Queen's Royal Regiment, who had been severely wounded during the raid died the following day. Work teams were organised to get Kenley back operationally as soon as possible. Rubble was poured into the numerous bomb craters that littered the runways and covered flat with rollers, so as to make it possible for aircraft to take-off and land. Some aircraft did manage to find a place to land, but others were directed to Redhill and Croydon.

No. 54 Squadron home based at Hornchurch had flown off earlier morning to operate from their forward base at Manston. Colin Gray, then a pilot officer remembers the squadron was extremely busy most of that day:

> Once again we went down to Manston, six of us led by George Gribble. We were scrambled at 10.54 am, against an unidentified aircraft which proved to be a Messerschmitt 110 on a reconnaissance; the poor fellow didn't have much chance. I was the first to fire, using up all of my ammunition from very close range, and knocking off large pieces, which slowed him right up; but four of the others in my squadron managed to have a squirt before he crashed into the sea. This aircraft was subsequently identified as a Me110 of 7(F) LG2 piloted by Oberleutnant Werdin who was killed, as was his radio/gunner. We landed back at Manston and were not ordered up again until 12.40 pm, when Squadron Leader Leathart led the whole squadron against a 300 plus raid over Kent.
>
> We encountered a large formation of Dorniers escorted by Me109s over Dover; during the action I was attacked by

another Spitfire, while using all my ammunition on a Dornier at 25,000 feet.

After the combat, we landed back at Hornchurch, which was fortunate for us, because our place at Manston was taken by No. 266 Squadron, who were also based at Hornchurch. Sure enough, Manston was once more attacked an hour or so later by Me109s. At 5.00 pm the squadron was again ordered off from Hornchurch to patrol Manston with 'Prof again leading. We were vectored north on to a raid of 250 plus, approaching the Essex coast. This included 51 Heinkel 111s bound for North Weald, and 58 bound for Hornchurch airfield. They had a combined escort of about 150 Me109s and 110s.

We arrived off Clacton-on-Sea, to find a squadron of Hurricanes already on the scene. I saw 'Prof Leathart being harassed by several Me 110s, so I fired at two, who lost interest in a hurry, and then at another, which 1 shot down. This fell into the middle of Clacton, fortunately without causing damage or injury to any civilians on the ground. The aircraft buried itself and its crew in the middle of Smith's Sandpit. It was still there, buried, when I paid a visit to England in 1978. The Me110 belonged to 4/ZG26, and was piloted by Hauptmann Ludtke, with gunner Unteroffizier Brillo; it crashed at 5.30 pm.

Hawker Hurricanes of No. 85 Squadron led by Squadron Leader Peter Townsend were hurriedly scrambled from Debden to patrol at 10,000 feet over Folkestone at 5.24 pm. A huge formation was picked up consisting of 150 to 200 aircraft. The formation was layered with Junkers Ju87s at 10,000 feet, Heinkels at 12,000 and above them Junkers JU88s and escorting Bf110s and 109s.

It seemed a hopeless task for the thirteen Hurricane pilots of 85 Squadron against such overwhelming numbers. Townsend led his colleagues into attack, eight miles east of Foulness Point. As they went into the attack, some of the German bombers separated and individual combats commenced. The German fighters now also became involved in the melee. One pilot flying that day was Pilot Officer Frank Walter-Smith, this was to be his first action and his combat report relates his individual battles:

> I picked out a Messerschmitt 110 and after about one and half minutes of steep turning, I delivered a frontal attack on it from a height of 2,000 feet above, opening fire at 100 -150 yards. It was a good burst of four seconds and I saw smoke coming from both engines as it glided down from 8,000 feet to strike the sea about 40 miles out. After giving other various enemy aircraft some short bursts, I delivered another frontal attack on a 110, which broke up at about 3,000 feet. The rear gunner or pilot baled out. This attack took place at 5,000 feet, about 60 miles due east of Margate. The aircraft broke up making a series of splashes in the sea.

The squadron was in the very forefront of the action and over the next two weeks in August of the eighteen pilots, 14 of them would be shot down within that fortnight and one of those would be Frank Walker-Smith.

Weather on Tuesday 20th August curtailed any real enemy action during the morning with only a few reconnaissance aircraft observed over the Straits of Dover and towards the Thames Estuary. During the afternoon however, at 2.45 pm radar alerted the controllers at Fighter Command of a large assembly of aircraft over Calais estimated at 190 aircraft strong.

Fighters were scrambled and met the enemy formation, which had crossed the coast between Manston and Dover. As the Germans entered over the Thames Estuary, they were met by stiff opposition and five of their aircraft were destroyed and others damaged. The airfield at Manston was attacked again an hour later, when a formation of 12 Messerschmitt 109s made a strafing attack, but they were driven off by the ground defence guns and soon disappeared from whence they came.

It was on this day also, that Prime Minister Winston Churchill delivered a speech in the House of Common's that would forever associate the sacrifice and bravery that the pilots of Fighter Command were undertaking day after day to defend the skies over Britain. Churchill in his speech also honours the aircrews of Bomber Command:

> 'The gratitude of every home in our Island, in our Empire, and indeed throughout the world, except in the abodes of the guilty, goes out to the British airmen who undaunted by odds, unwearied in their constant challenge and mortal danger, are turning the tide of world war by their prowess and by their devotion.
>
> Never in the field of human conflict was so much owed by so many to so few.'
>
> All hearts go out to the fighter pilots, whose brilliant actions we see with our own eyes day after day; but we must never forget that all the time, night after night, month after month, our bomber squadrons travel far into Germany, find their targets in the darkness by the highest navigational skill, aim their attacks, often under the heaviest fire, often with serious

Airfields and Radar come under attack

loss, with deliberate careful discrimination, and inflict shattering blows upon the whole of the technical and war making structure of the Nazi power.

On no part of the Royal Air Force does the weight of the war fall more heavily than on the daylight bombers who will play an invaluable part in the case of invasion and whose unflinching zeal it has been necessary in the meanwhile on numerous occasions to restrain.

During the afternoon of 24th August, North Weald aerodrome in Essex suffered its first heavy mass raid. At 3.40 pm, eight Hurricane fighters of No. 151 Squadron were hurriedly scrambled; their new commanding officer Squadron Leader Eric Bruce King had only arrived at the squadron some forty minutes earlier. Once airborne they were vectored to a German raid approaching from the east. The enemy formation consisted of thirty to fifty Dornier 17s accompanied by up to 100 Heinkel 111's and Messerschmitt 110's, stepped up three sections, line astern at 15,000 feet heading towards the base. More than 200 bombs were dropped starting from the western part of North Weald village, then through the aerodrome itself. Many buildings were hit and damaged including the officers and airmen's married quarters and a power house. Casualties included nine men of the 7th Battalion Essex Regiment, who were tragically killed when their air-raid shelter suffered a direct hit. Ten other personnel were also injured. Those killed were buried at the local church of St. Andrews.

The 151 Squadron Hurricane aircraft from North Weald harassed the German bombers and claimed three Heinkel 111s destroyed as well as two Messerschmitt Bf109s damaged. One Hurricane was forced to crash-land damaged back at base; Pilot Officer Irving Smith, a New Zealander was uninjured. The new commanding officer flying

Airfields and Radar come under attack

Hurricane V7389, had his airscrew shot off in combat with the Messerschmitt 110s, but he too landed safely.

Eric Clayton was serving with 56 Squadron ground crew at the time of the raid:

> Our dispersal area was on the far side of the airfield and we decided it was time to take cover. A small slit trench was to hand covered with sandbags with an entrance at each end. About five or six of us dived into it. In the dark we heard the exploding bombs approach relentlessly, at ordered intervals. The words 'stick bombing' flashed through my mind and immediately 'would the intervals match our slit trench or not? Two thuds away and I was sweating (were my friends?), one thump away and then nothing!
>
> That last bomb had landed very close to the trench and we were stunned by the impact of the explosion. I came to in the dark aware of an acrid smell of cordite. There was a glimmer of light above and I clambered towards it, pulling myself up through the soil into the bright sunlight. By now two of the others had 'come to' and were following me. I looked at what remained of the trench and, at the other end, there was a pair of legs thrashing the air wildly; then there were muffled shouts. I quickly ran to the waving legs, pulled aside two sandbags - which were riddled with shrapnel - and helped by the others, heaved him out of the ground. A rather pale face with a shock of blond hair appeared; he was a ground crew colleague, a tall, quiet and friendly Irishman.
>
> We had been preoccupied with our own predicament; as I looked about me, I

114

could see that North Weald had received a battering. Immediately before me, the airfield was badly cratered - including a line of craters leading to our slit trench! Though the runway seemed OK. But on the far side where the station buildings were, there was much damage; a pall of dust hung over it and there were fires from which black smoke arose.

We could only watch as the station came to life after this pounding - figures appeared out of the dust cloud, the fire tender moved off to deal with the fires, organised group appeared with shovels to fill in the craters - whilst we awaited the returning aircraft. Amazingly, the aircraft hangars, where major repairs and inspections were carried out, were undamaged. However, we later learned that nine soldiers had been killed in a shelter which had received a direct hit. Some of us in B Flight had good reason to be thankful for the 'near miss'.

On that same day, 56 Squadron also appointed a new commanding officer, Herbert Moreton Pinfold to lead them into battle. When interviewed he related his memories of that time:

> I took command of 56 Squadron at North Weald on 24th August, when the battle was at its height. The squadron had suffered quite a few casualties and both flight commanders had been killed before my arrival, which was bad; I knew I had an important job to do and I was determined to lead by example.
> The first five days were very intense indeed; I flew fourteen sorties, three of

Airfields and Radar come under attack

them in one day with only eight pilots available. The following week, the squadron was so depleted that we had to renew our losses with foreign pilots; the Czechs and Poles.

The Germans undertook their most audacious and deepest raid into Essex, attacking the aerodrome at Debden on the 26th August, when six Dornier bombers with fighter escort were able to avoid the fighter defence. They dropped their bombs, but little damage was achieved. On their return trip however at 3.35 pm, they were intercepted by Hurricanes of No. 310 Czechoslovakian Squadron based at Duxford and on its first operational flight. The Czechs on seeing the German crosses and Swastikas were eager to repay the brutality and cruel occupation of their mother country. They immediately went in to attack and claimed three enemy destroyed although in return they suffered due to inexperience and as a result three of their own aircraft were lost including their CO's P3887, although they suffered no pilot casualties. No. 1 Royal Canadian Squadron also chased the fleeing raiders, but took losses in return, three Hurricanes shot down with one of the pilots killed. Leading the Czechs that day was Squadron Leader George Blackwood; his combat report relates his action:

> A large formation of enemy aircraft came in from the coast. Dorniers sighted near North Weald flying in Vics of three, line abreast. I dived in from astern and opened up at 600 yards but drew back due to intense return fire from enemy gunners. At approximately 12,000 feet I saw a Dornier slightly apart from the others, so I decided to attack this one. I went in from astern at 300 yards and fired two long bursts. The bomber shuddered and began descending either trying to take evasive action or appearing out of control.

116

Airfields and Radar come under attack

At that moment, I smelt burning and realised my starboard wing was blistering, indicating my fuel tank was ablaze inside. I broke off the attack as the tank began flaming and at once decided to bale out. I undid my straps and disconnected the oxygen tube and at the same time turned my aircraft on its back and dropped out. I landed safely in a field unhurt and walked to the nearest house which was a farm cottage.

On 28th August 1940, No. 603 'City of Edinburgh' flew down to 11 Group to take up operations at Hornchurch. Among those who arrived with the squadron was a young South African named Gerald Stapleton; he remembers the intense action that was to greet the newly arrived pilots:

We arrived at Hornchurch in late August and we went into action almost straight away, it was utterly hectic. Our dispersal had air-raid shelters nearby and we would sit around our Nissan hut and could scramble into our aircraft in about a minute from the hut. I remember 'Uncle' George Denholm our commanding officer getting into his Spitfire and getting airborne long before any of us, although he was older. We found out his secret, he didn't strap himself in before he took off; he'd just jump in, start up and get into position to take-off and then he would strap up, while we were still trying to catch up.

We only used to wear leather flying jackets; we didn't bother with Sidcot suits or anything like that. We use to leave our flying helmets over the spade grip in the cockpit and parachutes in the seat; so all

117

we had to do was strap it on, once you were in then away we'd go.

The day Hornchurch was bombed, the bombs hit the north-east corner, where some of the buildings were, but this was only minor. The flight-path was holed quite badly, but there was a short area which one could land on, at the southern edge of the airfield. A Junkers 88 did come over and bomb that little bit, but within 24-hours the aerodrome was fully operational again, because the whole station turned out to fill in the bomb holes.

The squadron had been up during the attack and we were given instructions to land at our satellite airfield at Rochford. I remember being caught on the ground at Rochford a couple of days later, when we saw twelve Heinkel's coming over and we watched them until the bombs started to fall; then we raced for the shelters. There were twelve mock Hurricane aircraft sited on the north side of the airfield and they got hit quite badly.

The 29th August was to be a bad day for Frank Walter-Smith. His squadron, No. 85 was scrambled late afternoon and he along with eleven other colleagues were told to patrol over Hawkinge. At approximately 4.00 pm, they sighted 18 enemy bombers with an escort of 30 Bf109 fighters. They were at a height disadvantage and had to climb to attack. As they were just about to engage they sighted a much larger formation between Beachy Head and Hastings. As their leader, Peter Townsend tried to manoeuvre his pilots into a better position; they were attacked from above and behind.

Walter-Smith's Hurricane was hit by bullets and cannon shells and he was wounded in the right foot. He immediately took evasive action to try and avoid making himself a further target, he pulled his control column forward and went into a dive, but he found his aircraft did not respond to the rudder controls or throttle. He had no other choice but to bale out, which he did from a height of 16,000 feet. He gently floated down without further incident and landed at Hawkhurst, Kent. He was attended too and transported to Etchingham where they operated on his injured foot, having to lose the little toe. He returned to the squadron later that evening.

Although he survived the Battle of Britain, Walter-Smith was to lose his life in a flying accident on 13th March 1941 with two other pilots, Flight Lieutenant Sammy Allard and Pilot Officer William Hodgson, when their Havoc monoplane crashed and burst into flames shortly after take-off.

Iain Hutchinson was a sergeant pilot serving with No. 222 Natal Squadron based at Hornchurch; he remembers the courage that the ground crews displayed during one of several attacks against the aerodrome:

> The airfield was under attack and chunks of shrapnel were raining down. When I taxied my Spitfire towards the dispersal, no one could be seen; they had all taken cover in the air-raid shelters. Before I rolled to a halt and cut the engine, I was suddenly aware of 'B' Flight ground crew, under the command of the flight sergeant swarming around my aircraft. The fuel bowser was racing out to refuel my aircraft, while the armourers laden with ammunition were reloading the guns. The noise from the explosions going on around us was terrifying, but not one of those magnificent men faltered for a moment in their tasks. I was frankly relieved to be taking off again.

Airfields and Radar come under attack

'B' Flight mechanic Jack Shenfield of 54 Squadron also remembers the raids on Hornchurch:

> At the time, we had just got our aircraft away when the bombs started falling, and I ran towards the shelter. What I also remember well, was that there was an ack-ack unit or gun emplacement near to our dispersal. There was so much dust being thrown up by the bombs and the guns were firing, but it made me wonder how these people could see what they were firing at. Once I got to the shelter, we were all packed in there and the sergeant closed the door. We had only been in there a minute or so, when there came a loud banging on the door. The sergeant opened the door and there stood the driver of the bowser; this was the vehicle that carried all the high-octane aviation petrol for the aircraft. He had parked just outside the shelter with all of the bombs falling all around. The sergeant in no kind manner told him 'Sod off and take that bloody thing with you and park somewhere else before you blow us all to pieces.' This he did before they would let him into the shelter.

Joe Crawshaw was an airframe rigger in the same squadron as Iain Hutchinson and was one of those servicing the Spitfires under fire as they returned from combat:

> I certainly recall that before the air-raid siren had sounded the all clear, some of our aircraft were beginning to return and were managing to avoid the bomb craters; but one or two of them had stopped suddenly in the middle of the flight-path,

having run out of fuel. A corporal and myself jumped into a lorry; one of us grabbed some rope and we went out on to the airfield to tow the stranded aircraft away, leaving room for others to land. There were some casualties that day, just near our dispersal. There was a truck standing near the perimeter track which appeared to be abandoned, but when we looked, the men inside were dead.

WAAF Signals Operator Joy Caldwell was working in the Operations Room at Hornchurch, when they came under attack on 31st August. She was just eighteen at that time and remembers vividly the raid:

I will always remember that raid as it was on the date of my father's birthday. My friend Joan and I were on duty and the Ops Room had received information of one hundred plus formations coming in. Our controller Ronnie Adams told us to put our tin hats on, but some had already done this. The building was sand-bagged all around and we felt quite secure, but when the bombs started to drop and things began to rattle and bang and begin falling down, it got to be unpleasant. I don't think we were ever frightened because we were too ignorant; we didn't realise what could happen.

The biggest raid came over at lunchtime; they really did paste us then. I think they dropped something like sixty bombs on us, and I think three airmen were killed. We were walking back to our billets when they came over again at teatime. I was walking across the parade ground, when suddenly one of the German aircraft

began to strafe; as the bullets hit the
ground I dashed across the parade ground
as fast as my legs would carry and hurtled
myself through one of the barrack block
double doors and found myself lying on
the floor of one of the airmen's billets. I
managed to pick myself up off the floor,
somewhat dishevelled, while a number of
sleepy-eyed airmen wondered what all the
fuss was about.

Hornchurch came under attack three times during that day,
but miraculously remained operational. No. 54 Squadron's
Operations Book gave a clear picture of the second raid:

A really amazing day. Hornchurch
bombed. The miraculous escape of three
of our pilots, who were bombed out of
the planes. The station bombed a second
time.
At 1.15 pm a large formation of enemy
bombers – a most impressive sight in Vic
at 15,000 feet – reached aerodrome and
dropped bombs (probably 60 in all) in a
line from the other side of our original
dispersal pens to the petrol dump and
beyond into Elm Park. Perimeter track,
dispersal pens and barrack block windows
suffered, but no damage to buildings
caused and the aerodrome in spite of its
ploughed condition remained serviceable.
The squadron was ordered off just as the
first bombs were beginning to fall and
eight of our machines safely cleared the
ground; the remaining section however,
just became airborne as the bombs
exploded. All three machines were wholly
wrecked in the air. The survival of the
pilots is a complete miracle. Sergeant

Airfields and Radar come under attack

Davis, taking off towards the hangars, was thrown back across the River Ingrebourne two fields away, scrambling out of his machine unharmed.

Flight Lieutenant Deere had one wing and his prop torn off; his machine was turned over and came down and slid along the aerodrome for a hundred yards upside down. He was rescued from this unenvious position by Pilot Officer Edsall, the third member of the section, who had suffered a similar fate, except he had landed the right way up. Dashing across the aerodrome with bombs still dropping, he extracted Deere from his aircraft. 'The first and last time, I hope' was the verdict of these truly amazing pilots – all of whom were ready for battle again the next day.

Although the aerodrome had suffered, in the air, the squadrons had had some measure of success against the enemy raiders. Sergeant John Norwell claimed five enemy aircraft and later when interviewed gave a good insight into the daily rigors of a fighter pilots day:

That Saturday was certainly a fine day. It started as most days for a fighter pilot, up with the dawn. We were up at quarter past four. I felt in my bones that it was going to be a good day. We were in the air just after 5 pm and patrolled again shortly before 8.30 am, looking for enemy raiders approaching from the south coast of France. We saw three or four waves of Junkers 88s protected by a bunch of Bf109s above them. We were flying at 15,000 feet, between the bombers and the fighters. The fighters did not have much

123

chance to interfere with us before we attacked the bombers. I selected the end bomber of the formation, which numbered between fifteen to eighteen; I gave this Junkers a burst of fire lasting only two seconds, but it was enough. It broke away from the formation and dived down. I saw it crash into the sea.

Suddenly I immediately noticed a Messerschmitt fighter diving after me. I throttled back and he overshot. He was now about 150 yards in front and he now presented a beautiful target. I fired short bursts into him and he immediately began to smoke and dived away, plummeting into the sea. The sky which had been full of aircraft was now clear, so I decided to head home for breakfast.

In fact I didn't get any breakfast at all on my return, I only had time for a hot drink before we were ordered to stand-by again and by 11.30 that morning, we were off again.

During this patrol, we were attacked by about a dozen 109s and we broke and began to deal with them individually. I had a dog-fight with one; both of us trying to get in a position to outmanoeuvre the other. I eventually got on to his tail and he made off towards the French coast. We raced across the Channel like mad. As we neared the French side, I let him have it and then he began to go down; I saw him crash into a field. I headed for home without further contact with the enemy. I carefully examined my Spitfire when I landed, certain that I must have been hit somewhere, but no, not a mark.

Airfields and Radar come under attack

Our third show of the day began just before 4.00 pm. We were flying towards the Thames Estuary at 5,000 feet, when I saw anti-aircraft shells bursting in the sky towards the north-east. We changed course and began to climb for a place where we thought we should meet the enemy. We did. They were flying at 12,000 feet, twenty Junkers 88s in tight formation accompanied by twenty 109s above them. They were flying towards London and we could see the balloon barrage shining in the sunlight.

When we spotted the fighters we pulled up to meet them. I managed to get under a 109 and fired two short bursts and smoke started to pour out of him and he went down out of control. Suddenly, tracer bullets started whizzing past my machine. I turned sharply to see another 109 attacking one of our pilots. I turned on the attacker and fired; he immediately began to slow down and began to smoke. Soon the whole aircraft was enveloped in flames and pieces of airframe began to fly off. As it tumbled down towards the Thames, it was really a bunch of blazing fragments instead of a whole aircraft. It was an amazing, but terrifying sight.

Biggin Hill suffered a number of raids over the period of 48-hours on the 31st August and 1st September, the worst damage being inflicted during the late afternoon of the 31st. The following account was given by Felicity Hanbury, an Assistant Section WAAF Officer serving on the aerodrome when the raids occurred:

It was a sunny morning and I was talking to my flight sergeant in the guard-room

Airfields and Radar come under attack

about the ordinary routine of the day, when the station broadcast ordered one of the squadrons to 'come to readiness.' I told her that I might as well stay where I was for the time being and then go with her to one of the airwomen's slit trenches nearby, should a raid occur. The minutes passed by, but there were no further announcements, soon I started off towards my office in the station headquarters building.

Biggin was a delightful station, surrounded by rolling hills and green fields broken by little woods of cedar and beeches. The gardens of the officers' mess looked neat and pretty and the ivy climbing up the outside walls made a perfect natural camouflage.

As I approached and entered the headquarters, the sirens began to wail and we were then told to go to the trenches. These were long rectangular concrete vaults, half underground and covered with mounds of earth. A few seconds later we heard one of our squadrons get into the air, then another, finally the civilian air-raid warning could be heard in the surrounding area. I glanced up at the sky and caught a glimpse of one of our squadrons, it was a comforting sensation.

We had hardly settled down, when the noise of the patrolling aircraft overhead changed from a constant buzz to the zoom and clatter of a dog-fight. Then things happened quickly. There was a terrifying head-splitting roar which grew louder and louder, completely drowning out the sound of the combat above. 'We are being dive-bombed' said someone who still had her voice. Most of the others sat quietly with their arms folded, but in one corner I noticed a girl with eyes closed who seemed to be whispering to herself. I learned later that she had been reciting the Lord's Prayer. An instant later, just as it seemed as if the noise couldn't become any more deafening without the aircraft coming through the top of the trench, bombs began crashing all around us. One landed a few feet away from the entrance to the trench. Its hot blast of air bowled us over like nine-pins and a shower of stones and chunks of earth poured down the steps of the shelter.

I remember thinking, 'I suppose this is how one feels during an earthquake.'

I was just beginning to feel my ears, eyes and limbs belonged to me again, when the whole terrible process started again. The terrific shuddering and deafening noise made me feel as if my body was falling to pieces.

Among others who were in our shelter was a fighter pilot who had been stationed at Biggin Hill previously. He had landed a few minutes before the raid to get some minor repair done to his aircraft before returning to his home base. To his disgust and fury at having to sit in the trench during the raid is something I shall never forget. He moaned 'bloody bad luck, that's what it is, why Jerry couldn't have at least waited until my crate was fixed? Here I am sitting like a ninny while my pals are up there having a go at him.'

Then there was a lull broken only by the sound of our aircraft returning to refuel and re-arm. A few minutes later a messenger arrived saying a trench had been hit on the edge of the aerodrome. The Padre and another Officer followed the airman to the scene of the disaster and I thought I had better go and see if the airwomen were alright in their trenches. All was now deathly silent. I climbed through debris and around craters back towards the WAAF guardroom. As I drew nearer there was a strong smell of escaping gas. The mains had been hit. Through the window somebody shouted to me, 'Put your cigarette out before you blow the place to bits.' I complied.

One bomb had fallen on the airwomen's trench near the guardroom, burying the women who were sheltering inside; I couldn't help thinking how lucky I had been not to wait to go into that trench when the station broadcast had given us the preliminary warning. Looking off to the right of the runway, I noticed one of the NAAFI girls being laid under a hedge. I started to go towards her, but was stopped by an airman who whispered, 'the poor girl is dead'. I asked how it had happened 'machine guns, I suppose' said the airmen, 'you had better come along now, there is important work to be done at the trench.'

The Station Warrant Officer called for volunteers, among them was the Officer's Mess Gardener a dear old man who used to bring us fruit from his garden in the village. They got to work quickly and as the civilian 'all clear' went, the trench was uncovered. We had prepared ourselves for an awful sight, half expecting to find most of the girls dead, but we were happily mistaken. One by one, the girls were dug out. Some were hardly recognisable because of the dirt and dust on their faces. Others were dazed, whilst others were badly cut and bruised, but all were alive save one.

Those who were unhurt were in excellent form. First they asked about the raid, then they wanted cigarettes and then they offered to help. The wounded were calm and exceptionally brave. My Flight Sergeant who had damaged her back, begged me not to stay with her as there might be someone who needed more help than she did. I heard later from a WAAF Corporal who was in the trench at the time, that they all had been blown by the blast into a jumbled heap. If there was any danger of panic in the trench it was quickly removed by the extraordinary performance of the flight sergeant. When she couldn't sit up, she exclaimed good naturedly, 'my heavens, I have broken my back!' A few seconds later she noticed an unnatural feeling in her mouth, she shouted 'I have broken my false teeth too!' The girls couldn't help but smile as she drew the pieces of her plate from her mouth one by one.

A few days later, I attended a service funeral at the nearby cemetery for the airwoman that had been killed. Even then we were not left in peace, the Luftwaffe came again forcing the civilian mourners to take cover in the surrounding hedges while the Padre continued the burial service. After a while I returned to headquarters to report to the station commander and was told that the WAAF

Airfields and Radar come under attack

Officer's Mess could not be used as there was a delayed action bomb in the garden. I along with two WAAF Cipher Officers went to pack up and collect some of our things as quickly as we could. That night we had to sleep in the station commander's house. After some food, we went over to the WAAF Cookhouse to see how things were going there.

The Airwoman's Mess was the only one which had not been damaged by the raid and I could see that we would have to do all the cooking for the station for a bit. On the way there, I saw something like a white pillow lying on the ground, and as I approached to pick it up a voice said out of the darkness 'I shouldn't touch that if I was you Miss; it's marking a delayed action bomb.' I thanked him very much and tried hard not to look as though I was walking any quicker than I had been previously. Eventually I arrived at the Cookhouse to find the airwomen cooking virtually in the dark, but to the eternal credit of the cooks, they produced some delicious smelling sausages and mash to an endless stream of men going past the service hatch.

At 8.30 a.m. the next morning, the alert went again and we were ordered once more to take cover, but nothing happened to us as the attack was driven off. I spent the day visiting the Cookhouse and sick quarters, arranging billets to accommodate the airwomen who had become homeless, arranging transport and visiting the injured in hospital. At 10 am while at the Cookhouse, there was another raid and once more we heard the roar and zoom of dog fights and the sound of bombs coming nearer. We laughed and joked in the trench and soon it was over and everybody was back at work as though nothing had happened.

Later that afternoon, as I was returning to the aerodrome with another WAAF officer we were caught in another attack and our choices of action were few. There was no time to get to a trench, so we hurriedly put on our tin hats and ran into a nearby wood. The edge of the wood was near a crossroads and as we ducked under the trees, a police bell-shelter opened and a policeman shouted, 'you had better come in here.' We did not hesitate but scrambled in quickly, it was a tight squeeze and I still don't know how we all got inside. Soon the foul air became almost unbearable, so we all decided to smoke; the struggle to get to our cigarettes couldn't have been more difficult had we been in straight jackets. The smoke only made the atmosphere even more nauseating. One bomb crashed near enough to shake the bell-shelter. Soon after we all began drinking tea out of the policeman's thermos bottle.

Once the noise had died down and the raid had ended, we emerged and by the time we reached the aerodrome, a fierce fire was seen raging in one quarter. All of us pitched in to help put the blaze out before it could spread and before darkness fell, as we didn't want to be a target for German night bombers. Whilst some of us manned the hoses and carried buckets of water, others looked after those that had received burns or did other necessary things. Over the two days of raids, buildings had been destroyed, telephone lines blown up and the aerodrome itself cratered. But for not one instant, did it cease to be operational. For this heroic work, three of my WAAF's were later awarded Military Medals.

For her own work and courage during the enemy raids, Hanbury was later awarded the MBE. The WAAFs who were awarded decorations for their bravery under fire at Biggin Hill during the raids were Sergeant Helen Turner and Corporal Elspeth Henderson who had remained at their telephone switchboards and had continued to keep the information lines working, although their building had been hit and they had been covered in debris. The third WAAF was Sergeant Joan Mortimer who in an earlier raid had been manning the switchboard in the armoury; she had emerged with a bundle of red marker flags to help the bomb disposal teams mark out the bombs that had failed to detonate around the aerodrome, with the distinct possibility that they could go off at any time.

Glen Duhig who was an orderly in the officers' mess gave his account of the raid:

> I was in charge of the Tannoy and telephone, which was located under the staircase in the hall. The station commander was Group Captain Grice and the squadrons were No. 32 and 610. On the day we were bombed I was going from the mess to the airmen's mess for my meal. I was walking alongside the medical officer, when he said 'Look at those Blenheims.' They turned out to be Heinkels.
>
> We ran like mad to the sick quarters, where a blast wall had been erected and as we went in a large bomb exploded in the

road alongside and this propelled us well into the building. Sometime after the attack, a German airman had been captured and brought into the mess. He was fed a good spread, but was extremely arrogant. He spat when introduced to the pilot that had shot him down.

He was detained in the guard room and Flying Officer John Stone requested that breakfast be given the next morning. I was detailed to do this and the following morning went to the guard-room with a pot of coffee and all the trimmings. I met the medical orderly who gave me a bottle of cascara, which is very good for constipation. I put it in the coffee for the German, which I gather he drank, I never found out the conclusion.

North Weald Aerodrome was hit again on Tuesday 3rd September, when a formation of thirty plus Dornier 17 bombers with an escort of fifty Messerschmitt Bf110 fighter-bombers appeared from the north-east at 15,000 feet that morning at 10.35 am. Pilot Officer Tom Neil was serving with No. 249 Squadron and remembers clearly the events that day at North Weald.

I was on the 'state' when we all came to readiness in the early morning of 3rd September. The weather was brilliant with little more than an early morning mist and I had a new aircraft, V7313. I thanked God that it wasn't an L or N series - I was fed up with them. 56 Squadron's aircraft were newer than ours, probably because they lost them a good deal more quickly! I had no particular feelings of excitement or concern, just the proper degree of eagerness.

Airfields and Radar come under attack

At 9 am the whole squadron was scrambled. I was in the leading section of three on John Grandy's right with Percy Burton on his left. We took off in a wild rush towards the east and I found the masts floating past my left shoulder whilst climbing up. Not so bad after all. Patrol Chelmsford, we were instructed. Enemy plots were building up - 20, then 40, then 50 plus! We were being positioned as a precaution.

We climbed hard, turning slowly, the whole squadron lifting, falling and leaning in slow motion. Everyone was together and in position. There was no cloud worth mentioning, but I was too busy keeping station to be scanning the horizon or be much concerned about the enemy. The plots were still building up it seemed. An unspoken thought; were we too early? And in the right place? Time would tell.

We wandered about lances levelled. Ready and waiting. Essex spread out beneath us – the River Blackwater, the east coast and to the south, the line of the Thames. The Huns seemed to be taking a long time though. Round once more, and again. We had been airborne almost an hour when the order to 'pancake' was given. What a sell! We dropped down quickly towards base. Well, at least we would have been in position if they had decided to come. Better than being too late.

We landed, taxied in quickly and the bowsers lumbered forward to hook up and began refuelling. My airscrew tottered to a standstill. Crew members clambered on the wing-roots. 'Everything all right,

sir? 'New faces, but eager and smiling.
'Fine!'

The Hurricane aircraft of No. 249 Squadron had only just landed from a previous sortie and were being hastily refuelled and prepared by their ground crews, when suddenly the airfield sirens sounded and warned of the approaching danger. Pilots hurriedly jumped into their aircraft, taking to the skies with what fuel and ammunition had been replenished and went off at full pelt to gain height and speed away from the raiders. Three Bristol Blenheims of No. 25 Squadron also took off in time and headed out in a westerly direction.
Tom Neil continues:

> 'Turn round quickly', was the urgent instruction. We needed no persuading. My own aircraft was full, but some of the others weren't when the air-raid siren began its banshee wail and our second scramble order came. 'Patrol base, this time'. Crikey! That didn't sound so good.
> I raced across the grass to my position on John Grandy's right. Then, full throttle, 3,000 revs, and off again. Wheels up - I didn't even look. Climbing like hell.
> The squadron was strung out. Cutting corners and catching up. Climb! Climb! Hell's bells! We couldn't climb any faster. My throttle lever at full stretch. Being up front I was all right, but thinking of the poor blighters behind!
> From Sector Control came, 'Fifty plus bandits approaching from the south-east. Angels 17.' We clawed our way up, my engine raging. Through 7,000 feet, 10,000 up to 12,000, flying roughly east.
> Then, above and at eleven o'clock position ack-ack fire; faint brown smudges

blossoming. A growing cluster of it. Everything in slow motion then, aircraft! In the middle of all the puffs, Huns! Oh, God! Masses of them! 'Tally-ho!' My eyes glued to them. Fascinated. Growing closer. Clearer now. Large ones in front and in the middle. Others like flies stepped up and behind. Thousands, it seemed and there were only twelve of us!

We were below them and to the south. The Blackwater was in the background and they were heading due west. We turned slowly to the left, climbing hard still. I could see them properly now; the bombers were Dornier 17s, the fighters Messerschmitt 110's. Forging steadily ahead through the flowering puffs of ack-ack. Taking no notice. Oblivious.

The commanding officer said in a tense voice, 'Steady Ganer Squadron', and I was aware that I was the outside aircraft on the right of the formation, looking up to my left towards the bombers and above and to the right of the 110s. The 110s were close now. Very close. I could see them clearly. Some sort of coloured markings on the nearest aircraft I was going to pass right underneath!

If they chose to come down now we were finished. Closer. Turning to the left still and going hard. But I couldn't hit any of the bombers from here! They were the important ones, to heck with the fighters! Right underneath now; I could reach up and touch them. Why on earth weren't they coming down? My head bent right back. One 110 suspended above me - I could feel its airscrews rotating. Then, wings flashing. My leader turned on his back, other aircraft diving. A moment of utter surprise and panic. Mustn't be left behind! I tumbled after them in pursuit. What was happening? Were we being attacked? I kept screwing my head around, but could see nothing. My Hurricane was dropping like a stone, dust rising from around my feet, my head pressed against the roof of the cockpit. Other aircraft to my left. Diving like hell, and then pulling out. Hurricanes! I joined them. But, I hadn't fired! I hadn't had time to fire!

Flight Lieutenant Robert 'Butch' Barton was caught on the ground when the Germans began their bombing on the aerodrome:

'Holy Christmas' everything was coming down on top of us, bombs etc and all I could see was the sky full of aircraft above. So I hurriedly jumped into my aircraft and took off into the maelstrom. The Germans were so busy trying to get home that they were not defending anything, just flying out; they had done their attack and were now homeward bound. Little did they know that they had a few enemy aircraft right in their midst and I managed to shoot at three of them quite seriously.

Tom Neil:

Over the RT came a voice from below. High pitched with excitement, but controlled. 'We've been hit Ganer Squadron, but we're all right.'
I looked over the side. To my surprise, we were directly over North Weald and far

below, the whole aerodrome was hidden beneath a huge, spreading grey-brown pall of smoke and dust. They'd bombed us! The airfield! The blighters had bombed our airfield! It never occurred to me that we might not be able to land on it.

By the time we were back in the circuit, much of the smoke and dust had disappeared. All that remained were scores of large molehills on the grass. There had been other damage too, and lives lost, but I was aware only of the need to get down and the business of finding space on which to land.

We flew in from the direction of the masts, in rough sections of three, and touched down across the concrete and on the grass, weaving gently between the bomb-holes. As they raced past, mostly to my left, I watched them quite dispassionately. There was no problem, no one was the least bit concerned and we all landed safely without incident.

This time the Luftwaffe scored substantial damage destroying hangars, the Operations Room block and a few aircraft, killing five and injuring another thirty-five. Although the damage was extensive, the aerodrome remained operational. A fireman from the local fire service who attended the aerodrome after the raid recalled:

On the Tuesday the aerodrome was bombed again, this time mid-morning. Epping Urban of course attended, but there was not much chance of liaison, as just about everything had been hit and there was much to do. We arrived whilst the water was still pouring out of the overhead tank. It had been machine gunned and looked like a colander. We were given the job of tackling an aircraft which was alight in the first hangar. There were three draw backs. Firstly the ammunition kept going off in the aircraft, secondly it was impossible to get more than 25 yards from an unexploded bomb, and thirdly the only water there to use was from the sewage septic tank, as all the mains had been blown up. This was kept replenished from lorries with 500 gallon canvas dams drawn in from as far afield as Brentwood. Only one delayed action bomb went off while we were there and all we got was covered in dirt. I suppose we must consider ourselves lucky it wasn't a lump of concrete. Just to complete the happy scene, the station Tannoy system which by some miracle was still working gave out the message 'Enemy aircraft approaching at 10,000 feet, anything is likely to happen any minute now'! The chap must have had a distorted sense of humour, fortunately for us the target wasn't North Weald.

The German raiders did not get away lightly for all their efforts; one Dornier 17 of 5/KG2 was shot down and crashed at Langenhoe, near Pyefleet Creek, two Messerschmitt Bf110s of I/ZG2 collided during the raid, one falling to earth at Rye Hill near Epping, the other crashing at Hobbs Cross Farm, Harlow. Another 110 was shot down and crashed at Stowmaries, while another crashed at Pudsey Hall Farm, Canewdon near Rayleigh.

Two days later the operations room was moved to a building at Marden Ash before eventually establishing at Blake Hall Mansion, just a few miles away.

Fortunately for Fighter Command, the German attacks against the aerodromes began to cease, following a reprisal

Airfields and Radar come under attack

raid by Bomber Command on Germany, who had a few nights previous bombed London by mistake.

This attack against German cities had outraged Hitler so much, that he had summoned Goring and instructed him to change his tactics, instead of RAF aerodromes, the bombing would now be turned against London. This decision would cost the Germans the battle. If the bombing of aerodromes had continued, there is no doubt that Fighter Command could not have continued as such, unless they had strategically moved their squadrons further north of the Thames. This brief respite from the bombing would now also allow Fighter Command to take stock and build up its losses and replenish aircraft and pilots.

CHAPTER 7

Der Angriff auf London
(The Bombing of London)

Saturday 7th September was a day, which would completely change the tide of the battle. Only several nights earlier, Prime Minister Winston Churchill had given Bomber Command explicit instructions to hit back at the heart of Germany, Berlin. Eighty-one Hampden twin-engine light bombers dropped their bombs on the German capital and other industrial targets including the Siemens factory. This raid was in reprisal for an attack made by the Luftwaffe on the previous night of the 25th August, when during a mission to bomb installations around the Chatham, Rochester and Thames Haven oil refineries, bombers of Luftflotte 2 had mistakenly dropped their bomb loads over central London. Areas hit during the night included Islington and Finsbury in north London, Stepney, Bethnal Green and East Ham in the East End.

The British reprisal had so outraged Hitler that he immediately ordered his Reichmarschall Hermann Göring to made immediate plans for the bombing of London, both by day and by night; thus bringing Britain to its knees and surrender terms. Hitler had spoken defiantly to his ardent supporters at the Sportsplatz in Berlin in response to the bombing of the German capital and told his captive audience:

> It is truly magnificent to see our folk at war and its total discipline. We realise this is all the more in a time when Mr. Churchill is demonstrating the use of his invention: the nightly air raid. He does not do this because air raids are particularly effective, but because his Air Force can't penetrate German airspace during the day.

Der Angriff auf London

While the German pilots, the German planes fly over English land day by day, no Englishman has managed to as much as cross the North Sea by daylight. That is why they come at night and drop their bombs; you know it well, indiscriminately and on civilian residents, farms and villages. Wherever they see a light, they drop a bomb.

I did not answer for three months because I was of the opinion that they would ultimately stop this nonsense. Mr. Churchill perceived this as a sign of our weakness. You will surely understand that now we are giving our answers night after night and this at an increasing rate.

The hour will come that one of us will crack and it will never be National Socialist Germany! And should the Royal Air Force drop two thousand or three thousand or four thousand kilograms of bombs, then we will now drop 150,000, 180,000, 230,000, 300,000, 400,000, yes one million kilograms in a single night. And should they declare they will greatly increase their attacks on our cities, then we will utterly erase their cities! We will put these nightmare pirates out of business, God help us!

Hermann Göring decided he would personally take full command of the planning for the attacks on London, over-ruling his main commanders Generalfieldmarschalls Albert Kesselring and Hugo Sperrle. Göring travelled to Calais in his own personal train to set up his headquarters and witness at first hand the aerial assault against London.

The weather that day dawned fine over the south-east although there was some mist over the Channel, but this soon cleared to give perfect flying weather. The morning saw little air activity apart from a few German reconnaissance aircraft sorties. At RAF plotting rooms there was no sign of enemy formations building up across the Channel over in France and squadrons were kept at readiness most of the day, waiting for the call to scramble.

At around 4.00 pm, alarm bells sounded when the radar stations began picking up formations forming over the Calais area of over twenty plus aircraft. The RAF commanders assumed that the raids would again head for targets such as airfields and installations and all fighters were scrambled to patrol these areas.

Göring in the meantime, had gathered his staff to a forward position overlooking the sea at Calais and viewed through his binoculars his vast armada of bombers and fighter escorts as they roared overhead towards the white cliffs of Kent and onwards towards their target, London. Vast formations stepped up at various altitudes consisting of over three hundred bombers and an escort of six hundred fighters headed out in two waves. The first formation would head for the Thames Estuary and the second would follow heading directly for London.

This caused confusion within Fighter Command as to the Luftwaffe's real targets and heading. All too soon and too late, it was recognised that London was the target and fighter squadrons had to be re-deployed urgently to cover the capital.

Those squadrons covering sector aerodromes were hurriedly despatched to try and intercept the bombers who were now closing in over London, preparing to drop their bombs. Some RAF fighters managed to intercept and engage, but they were heavily pressed by the Messerschmitt 109s and 110s that provided close escort from above and alongside their bomber comrades. On the run into London, the German aircraft ran the gauntlet of the anti-aircraft defences within and around the capital, sending up black puffs of flak across the summer sky.

Der Angriff auf London

Once over the target, the bombs rained down; first on the London dock area of Millwall, Silvertown and Limehouse and then further up towards Tower Bridge. Vast warehouses full of timber and sugar and other inflammable produce was set ablaze, causing the flames and smoke to be seen for miles and giving the incoming German air fleet a perfect beacon to guide them in.

More RAF fighters were now arriving on the scene and eager to get stuck into the enemy formations. At Cambridge, the Duxford Wing comprising of three squadrons of approximately thirty-four aircraft led by Squadron Leader Douglas Bader, had taken off at 4.45 pm with instructions to patrol the aerodrome at North Weald. While in this area at 15,000 feet, Bader and his men had noticed anti-aircraft shells bursting to the east and then sighted a huge formation of about one hundred aircraft heading north at 20,000 feet.

The RAF fighters were at a disadvantage being below the enemy formation, but climbed up to engage anyway. On attacking, Bader and his men were then attacked in turn by Messerschmitt 109s, who had been sitting up sun of the bombers, some 5,000 feet above. During the combat that followed several German aircraft were claimed destroyed.

On return to Duxford, Bader found his Hurricane was badly damaged due to the fight with the 109s; as was two other 242 Squadron pilot's aircraft, that of Sub-Lieutenant Richard Cork, who received slight injuries and Pilot Officer Denis Crowley-Milling who had to undertake a force-landing at a disused old airfield at Stow St. Maries, Essex; which wrecked his aircraft's undercarriage. No. 310 Czech Squadron also based at Duxford suffered one casualty, that of Sergeant Josef Koukal who was forced to bale out after being shot down. His aircraft had caught fire and he was badly burned. Another pilot, Sergeant Vilem Goth also was hit by enemy fire, but managed to bring his aircraft in to do a forced landing at Purleigh. He was unhurt.

Der Angriff auf London

Sergeant Pilot John Burgess was flying with No. 222 Squadron and clearly remembers the following events that happened that day:

> The most definitive incident that happened to me during this time took place on 7th September. We had a number of engagements during the day and we took off during the evening and got broken up by some 109s. We then proceeded independently and I chased some Dornier 215s over the Thames accompanied by a chap in a Hurricane. There were six Dorniers who were travelling down the Thames Estuary heading east back towards France. We began attacking when we were ourselves were attacked by six 109s that came down on us and we had to break away. I then proceeded to South London and as I approached I saw a formation of Heinkels which were heading home. Eventually, I managed to get about three miles behind the large formation which was having a lot of flak thrown up at it by our ground defences.
>
> As I was closing nearer, I suddenly noticed two aircraft in echelon which I thought were Hurricanes, so I thought I would join up with them and we could make a concerted attack together. As I pulled in to join them making a wide Vic formation about 150 yards, I looked over to see that they had yellow noses. I pulled in behind the leader, which put me in the right position and range to engage him; I opened up on him and he immediately

rolled on to his back and went down with white smoke streaming out.

The engagement started at about 17,000 feet, not terribly high; he kept diving down and I followed him down firing all the way. I suppose at the closest point I was about 50 yards behind him, I then suddenly realised that we were getting very close to the ground, we were diving almost vertically at full throttle.

At this point I was down to around 2,000 feet and he went straight on down and went into the ground; I pulled up and had a white out because of the strain of pulling my aircraft out of the dive, all the blood went from behind my eyes and I couldn't see a thing, it was just a white opaque view. It was very hard to estimate the speed I had been doing in the dive.

We were using a variable pitch propeller controlled at 3,000 revs, if you dived at a certain maximum speed, the stop never worked and the speed of the propeller increased, which increased the revs. I think the maximum permissible on a Spitfire was about 3,500 revs, I seem to remember that I was doing about 4,000. What my speed was in that dive was I don't know, I certainly think it must have been in excess of 450 mph; which in a Spitfire was a bit of a dangerous speed.

There was no wing bending; but very often in the Battle of Britain, there were a number of pilots I knew ended up with ripples on the wing root because of pulling out of steep dives. Eventually in a matter of seconds my sight came back and I can remember I was very shaken, because obviously I had killed a man and I had never killed anyone before and to me it was quite a traumatic experience.

I then found I was running short of petrol, so I set course for the north and the Thames and I was almost back to Rochford, when my engine failed, my fuel had run dry. As I approached the airfield I noticed some high power tension cables in my line of flight and I had to make up my mind whether to get over the top of them. I don't think I could have made Rochford aerodrome, it was just too far to glide, so I had to make up my mind whether to go down and force-land before the power cable or try and get over, then force-land.

I saw a field ahead and I thought it was better to land with enough flying speed to spare, than not enough, so I slipped away the height and did a steep side slip down to this field and landed on it. It had just been ploughed I think because there was just corn stubble on it. It was very dry and as I hit the ground the prop blades bent back and lots of dust was thrown up. I got out of the aircraft which by then was looking pretty bedraggled.

A crowd of people appeared and came over one of the fences to see if I was o.k. One little girl who was about fourteen came over to me and asked was this a Spitfire? So I replied 'yes it is'. She said 'we are saving for a Spitfire at our local village; we are saving for £5,000.' There was a scheme at the time called the Spitfire Fund. She continued 'I don't think that thing's worth £5,000.'

Der Angriff auf London

'Butch' Barton, No. 249 Squadron:

> I was very much afraid on take off, but I found that when we started to get up at high altitude and if you sighted the enemy, a lot of your fear disappeared, it was rather marvellous, because you think to yourself 'God, there they are, God you've had it boy, this is it'. There were a hundred of them at least, that to me was something unbelievable. We attacked and the first aircraft I shot at, it didn't do anything, it just stayed in formation. Then I tried another one and as it went down I followed him and I followed him all the way. I said to myself, 'this one I'm going to make sure goes bloody well down. This is a crazy business!'

John 'Killy' Kilmartin who earlier had fought in France, and afterwards was an instructor at the newly formed OTU's remembers his time with No. 43 Squadron and particularly what took place on 7th September.

> Towards the end of August, an old friend and flight commander of 43 Squadron, South African Caesar Hull, had been given the job as squadron commander, and he rang me up at Aston Down and asked me to join them at Tangmere. I was only with them for three weeks and the squadron was badly mauled during the big show on September 7th. Caesar was shot down and killed and also Dick Reynell who was the Hawker's assistant test pilot, he was on his last day with us before he was due to go back to Hawker's and he too was unfortunately killed. I was the

last senior officer left and I was given the task of taking what was left of the squadron, I think there were seven or eight of us; back up to Scotland to rest and reform.

No. 43 Squadron had been scrambled that late afternoon to intercept a large force of Dornier 17s with fighter escort. Caesar Hull was last reported diving into attack the bombers before being pounced on by the Messershmitt 109s. He fell with his aircraft and crashed within the grounds of Purley High School, Surrey. He was buried at Tangmere.

Fellow pilot, Australian born Richard Reynell was also a victim of the heavy German fighter cover and was also shot down, although he did manage to bale out of his aircraft, he fell dead at Blackheath.

No. 222 Squadron who were based at Hornchurch, one of the nearest aerodromes to London; had been scrambled and they engaged with the enemy at 6.00 pm. Sergeant Rainford Marland was in action and his combat report relates:

On the afternoon of the 7th September, at approximately 18.00 hours, I was on patrol with the squadron when we sighted and attacked a formation of enemy bombers. We were patrolling at 29,000 feet and the bombers were 5,000 feet below us.

I was at the tail end of line astern formation and as we went down, I saw Me109s coming in to attack me. I therefore turned off and regained height, when I saw one Me109 below me. I dived to attack him and closed to 400 yards at 17,000 feet. We were then south-east of Thames Haven and flying due east towards the sea. I opened fire at 400 yards and closed to about 150 yards firing all the while.

I followed the enemy machine down to 9,000 feet, when I had to break away as I was again attacked by Me109s.

As I broke away, the enemy aircraft was going straight down into the sea and volumes of black smoke was trailing behind him. The Me109 had a yellow nose and yellow wing tips. After my first burst of fire, no evasive action was taken by the enemy.

No. 249 Squadron was also in action during the early evening. Having taken off from North Weald, the squadron was soon in action against a formation of Dornier bombers. Sergeant Pilot John Bentley-Beard was flying Hurricane N2240, when suddenly his aircraft was hit and damaged severely. He had no option but to bale out and landed in a field near a housing estate. He observed a crowd of people running towards him, most of them armed with various weapons. They must have thought he was a German pilot. He took one look at these people and immediately started running for his life. As he ran through a hedge, he collided with a policeman and after both of them had picked themselves up, he explained who he was. The policeman was able to prove to the crowd that he was in fact a British pilot. It was later thought that his aircraft had been damaged by our own anti-aircraft defences.

Bentley-Beard said later 'I was more scared of that crowd than of all the dogfights I had been in.' He was given back his parachute and took it back to North Weald to be repacked. The same parachute was to save his life again the following month, when while in combat over North Kent on 25th October, he was shot down by 109s at midday and was wounded. He baled out again and landed and was sent to Pembury Hospital to be attended. This time the parachute had been torn, so Bentley-Beard decided to cut a piece off and he kept it as a souvenir. He recovered from his wounds and went on to become a commissioned officer and achieved ace status having shot down seven aircraft during the battle.

Nineteen year old Leading Aircraftsman Frank Clarke was serving with No. 234 Squadron based at Middle Wallop in Hampshire; he recalls one of the pilots who failed to return that day:

> My flight commander was an Australian, Flight Lieutenant Pat Hughes. He intercepted a Dornier 17 and as he closed in on the aircraft, it exploded with such force that it wrecked his Spitfire. Hughes baled out, but his parachute failed to open. In the same encounter, his squadron leader, Joseph O'Brian also died. Although a number of witnesses saw Hughes aircraft crash at Darks Farm, Bessel's Green, the wreckage remained in the ground for twenty-five years. Pat Hughes was awarded the Distinguished Flying Cross posthumously. He had destroyed 15 enemy aircraft in twenty-four days of intensive combat.

At approximately 8.00 pm, for some unknown reason and under whose orders cannot be accounted, the invasion codename 'Cromwell' had been signalled, meaning that the invasion by the Germans was under way. Many church bells were rung and local Home Guard units were alerted and instructed to set up road blocks and prepare to counter an attack by German parachutists. This of course did not materialise in any form.

No. 605 Squadron based up in Scotland at Drem had received orders to send them down south into 11 Group that day. Bob Foster, then a 20 year old pilot officer recalls:

Der Angriff auf London

> The squadron was called south on 7th September, we flew from Drem to Abingdon where we re-fuelled and then we flew into Croydon and that evening when we landed, the first sight we had was of London burning. It was quite frightening to realise what we were flying into.

As darkness drew in that evening, all one could see for miles around was the flow of the flames that lit up the night sky over London. Even as far as the Thames Estuary coast, people could make out the brightness in the night sky emanating from the capital of England.

The raids continued through the night until 5.00 am the next morning, causing death and destruction never witnessed before on mainland Britain. The bombing had killed 430 civilians and seriously injured 1,600 others. The Luftwaffe had dropped 330 tons of high explosive and 440 tons of fire starting incendiaries. The blitz on London had begun.

The following morning, Londoners emerged from their shelters to witness the devastation of burnt out and demolished buildings that once were their home and work places. But undaunted, life had to go on and the process of carrying on with normal life as best they could began.

German attacks against London on the 8th were very low key compared with the previous day; this was mainly due to bad weather. Small raids against RAF airfields were conducted during mid-morning against Detling, Gravesend and Hornchurch, but little damage was achieved as the Germans were forced to turn back due to attacks from numerous RAF fighters.

The Luftwaffe were more successful that evening, when a raid consisting of 200 bombers took off and proceeded to bomb the capital from 7.30 pm until 4.30 am the next morning. The bombing was severe, killing 400 and injuring over 700 civilians. These night raids continued, trying to break the spirit and resolve of the British people who watched as their city was blown apart piece by piece. The fire crews of the National Fire Service bravely fought the blazing infernos as local streets and roads were engulfed by the fires caused by German incendiaries and high explosive bombs.

On the 13th September, Hermann Göring and his commanders had arrived in Berlin to talk with Hitler and provide intelligence information showing how the operation was proving successful against the Royal Air Force and that the invasion was still viable. Reports suggested that the RAF were losing aircraft in combat at a ratio of 3 : 1. With these figures Fighter Command would be down to its last few squadrons and the air superiority that the Germans needed to launch their invasion without enemy air opposition would be granted. Unfortunately, Luftwaffe pilot claims of aircraft shot down were widely exaggerated and this would be their undoing.

Following the meeting held in Berlin with his commanders, Hitler decided to postpone the invasion until the 17th September; this would hopefully allow the weather over the Channel to become settled following the previous days, which had been showery and with much cloud. It would also give Göring's Luftwaffe a few extra days to achieve full air superiority and wipe out the remaining RAF fighters.

On 14th, three raids developed during the afternoon when at 3.00 pm radar picked up aircraft heading across the Channel and crossing the English coast between Dungeness and Deal in Kent. The enemy was intercepted and combat met, with losses to both sides resulting in 11 RAF fighters being written off, two pilots killed and six wounded. The Luftwaffe lost ten.

One of those lost during combat that day was Sergeant Sidney Baxter serving with 222 Natal Squadron. He had taken off that afternoon from Rochford airfield near Southend and during combat with the enemy his Spitfire had been damaged. He struggled to get his aircraft back to base. Arthur 'Dave' Davis was an engine mechanic with the squadron and he recalls what happened next:

> We were watching our aircraft returning, waiting for our own particular Spitfire. Suddenly, Sergeant Baxter's Spitfire appeared and you could see straight away that he was in trouble. His tail plane was very badly shot up, and he was valiantly trying to land. He had just crossed over the airfield boundary hedge at a height of 50 feet, when the whole tail plane structure just dropped off. His aircraft just turned over and went straight into the ground. There was nothing anyone could do. It was a great shame as he was a very nice gentleman. He had earned the nickname of 'Clot' after forever questioning his ground crew about his Spitfire; when they asked him why he was always checking up, he would reply that he was the 'Clot' who had to fly the aircraft, after they had serviced it.

Brian Kingcome a flight lieutenant with No. 92 Squadron was over Canterbury at 22,000 feet that evening at 7.30 pm, when he led his squadron into attack on one of the German raids:

> I was leading the squadron and was vectored into the path of the approaching 'Bandits'. We were still climbing on our vector when I saw several formations of Messerschmitts passing directly over us in the opposite direction about 5,000 feet above us. There appeared to be no bombers, so I turned about and was climbing after the 109s, when I noticed another formation of enemy fighters

diving on to another squadron of Spitfires which was following us. The Spitfires apparently did not notice them, so as I turned and dived into the 109s, I gave the first one a two second burst with three quarter deflection and it turned away in a gentle spiral glide to the right and went into some cloud below.

I gave another chap a two second burst and the aircraft pulled up vertically on its back and fell away. I was then attacked by several Germans, but I escaped into cloud. When I climbed back again, I could not find the 'Bandits', so I returned to base.

Weather conditions forecast for the next day, the 15th September looked very promising, predicted fine with some cloud. This day would see the largest attacks against London in the prelude to an invasion.

CHAPTER 8

Diary of a Fighter Pilot

The following extracts are taken from the diary of a young Battle of Britain fighter pilot, Pilot Officer James Reginald Bryan Meeker who served with No. 249 Squadron at North Weald during the battle. Sadly he was killed on 27th September 1940, aged 21 years, having been credited with destroying six enemy aircraft. That day he had shared in the destruction of a Messerschmitt Bf 110 and was attacking a Junkers Ju88, when his aircraft was damaged by return fire from the bomber. He was forced to vacate his Hurricane aircraft P3834, but his parachute failed to deploy and he fell to his death. His body was found at Warren Field, Brightling Park. His aircraft crashed into the ground at Brake Field, Giffords Farm, Dallington.

On 8th October, he was posthumously awarded the Distinguished Flying Cross. He now rests in peace at West Dean Cemetery, Sussex.

September 2nd 1940

First day at our new station. Leapt from our virgin couches at 6.50 am. This shook me a bit. Was still slightly dopey when at 15,000 feet when we sighted a large lump of blitz. Solid block of twenty Dornier 215s with a large fighter escort.

Attacked en'masse then dived away as fighters came down. Joined 'Butch' again after a frantic tail watching break away and started after the bombers again. Suddenly we see a Dornier coming towards us, running for home. We jump on it 'Butch' sits on its tail pumping lead into it. I do quarter attacks. He doesn't like this, lumps start falling off and smoke pours out. I am awake now and feeling hungry. 'Butch' says: 'Don't waste any more ammunition on him, this guy is finished.' I say 'OK, Bud.' And formate on the Dornier, as he heads for Rochford. He is a wreck-rudder in ribbons and pieces falling off all the time. 'Butch' and I are very cocky, go home and shoot a horrid line.

Two more quick sorties seeing nothing and then more Blitzkrieg on the fourth do. We run into a whole pile of Me110s and Dorniers. Too far to attack the bombers, so we start mixing it with the 110s. They circle and a lot come down vertically behind us. I lose 'Butch' and everybody else as I turn round and round watching my tail.

Then a 110 rears up in front of me, plan view; as he does a steep turn. Range is almost point blank as I turn inside and plug him. He disappears under my nose and when I see him again he is diving vertically, starboard engine and wing blazing.

We sleep very soundly.

September 4th

Two patrols – 9.20 and 12.30, but no contact made and no fun at all. Just roaming around looking for the 'Hun in the Sun.' Watched night bombers in the dark, parachute flares and anti-aircraft bursts all over the sky. Slept well.

Diary of a Fighter Pilot

September 6th

Up in the morning over the Thames
Estuary to meet another raid. We nip in
before the Hun fighters can get at us and
we do a quick flank attack. Fighters follow
at once. I follow behind the bombers,
watching two Me109s coming up behind.
Before they get into range, I turn sharp
left and whip under them. Unfortunately
C....., who is following me, gets plugged
by one of these guys and has to crash-
land. I get into a circle with two 109s and
shoot at the second. He starts to dive so I
pull the plug and chase him. Third burst
sets him on fire, whole of starboard wing
and fuselage.

We are down to 500 feet, so I leave him
to burn and climb to 10,000 feet at full
bore. Fighting is still going on and two
more 109s come for me. They work in
pairs and it seems fairly easy to get
Number 2.

Again I pick him out and we tear down
at nought feet. We race along the
'Pilgrims' Way and I fire the rest of my
ammunition into him. Both radiators
stream glycol and I can smell him burning.
I formate on him when I finish my
rounds, and he has his oxygen mask off
looking out at me. I leave him to go home
and see him crash-land a few miles on.
Going home I see a parachute and circle it
– a British one. Later it turns out that it is
the C.O. who got shot down by 109s.

Diary of a Fighter Pilot

September 7th

I have the rest of the day off and a very good thing too. Squadron gets into the big London raids and loses quite a few. F……..died in hospital, W………. missing, several more shot down and baled out. S………and I drove down to Maidstone Hospital to pick up the CO. Coming back we get into Blackwall Tunnel, when the trouble starts raining down all around us – no time to get to a shelter. We stand under an arch and watch the bombers approaching in waves, hear the bombs whistle down and then the explosions. Molotov breadbasket showers incendiaries round us, several in gasworks, which fortunately does not go up.

The CO feels a bit hard done by as he's been shot down and wounded yesterday, then gets bombed today. S…… drives like a demon along a street and skids to a stop. Bus driver pulls up beside us and says 'Come on, nah turn it up mate – you're on the blinking floor this time.'

September 15th

The best day we've had. We go off at lunch time with another squadron and meet sixteen Dorniers and lots of 109s. We go into the bombers but 'Butch' breaks early as he gets hit. I break with him, lose him, then I go for the bombers again.

Meet them coming home and no 109s in sight. So I attack one on the edge of the formation. Get him straight away and he leaves the rest of the boys. Follow him, plugging all the time.

A quarter-attack comes off beautifully; see bullets going in, in a line from the nose back to the tail, at intervals of a foot all the way down. Dornier is smoking like a chimney and pieces fly past me. Then three blasted Spitfires horn in and drive me away from my own private and personal Dornier. One guy bales out from the Jerry. He has his arms folded and seems quite resigned. His ship crashes in flames and Spitfires shoot a line all round it, probably dropping visitors cards – 'I did this myself, see you in the brasserie 8.30 Saturday,' kind of thing.

Afternoon brings even better pickings. Again we attack Dornier formation and break it wide open. They scatter all over the sky and go for the clouds. I get one straight away with a long burst. He catches fire and goes straight in. I chase another one in and out of clouds, port engine catches fire and 'Butch' and I claim him as probable; damned sure he was finished?

Most successful day for the squadron, a bag of ten destroyed, thirteen probable and others damaged. Our losses nil. My bag – two destroyed, one probable and one damaged. Beginning to shoot a bit of a line. Celebration in the evening.

CHAPTER 9

Height of Battle -15th September 1940

The 15th September is now commemorated as the day in which the Royal Air Force turned the tide of the Battle of Britain against the mighty German Luftwaffe. In reality, to many pilots in Fighter Command it was just another day that brought anxiety, fear and the probability that many of them would not survive another day; which rushed through their minds while waiting for the call to scramble once more.

Flight Lieutenant 'Butch Barton stationed at North Weald remembers clearly an officer came in to the mess the night before the 15th, and told those who had gathered there the following information:

> On 14th September, we were told 'this is your last day, next day we expect the invasion to occur.' That was not very encouraging. We have come this far and this is where we are. I said to my fellow comrades, 'I'll tell you fellows, as soon as we are off duty tonight, I'm into the bar pretty quickly, I'm going to get myself a good few glasses of beer.'

On that day the pilots were up early as usual and at readiness waiting for instructions to get airborne from their various group controllers. The weather that morning was ideal with clear visibility, perfect flying weather. Strangely, no enemy activity had been observed and by 10.00 am, Fighter Command Headquarters wondered what the Germans were planning next. However news was relayed to Sector Stations from RAF Headquarters at 11.33 am that radar had picked up German aircraft gathering over the south-east of Boulogne, turning out across the Channel heading for the English coast between Dover and Folkestone. Immediately fighter squadrons in 11 Group were scrambled to intercept the threat. The Duxford Wing was called into action soon afterwards and instructed by control to patrol over the Gravesend and Canterbury line.

Charlton Haw 504 Squadron

> The day started early and by the late morning our squadron had been scrambled and we sadly lost four aircraft that day. During the morning engagements Ray Holmes brought down a Dornier which crashed close to Buckingham Palace, before he had to bale out himself. Pilot Officer John Gurteen was killed; he had trained with me at Sealand. His aircraft was seen diving out of control and he crashed onto a house at Longfield in Kent. Flying Officer Michael Jebb was also shot down that day during combat; he managed to get out of his Hurricane, but suffered terrible burns and succumbed to his injuries, dying a few days later.

For Sergeant Ray Holmes it would be a day he would never forget and would link his name forever in Battle of Britain history.

No. 504 were ordered to patrol London and at approximately 12.10 pm they sighted and attacked a formation of 20 Dornier 215s at 20,000 feet over the capital. As the German bombers sighted the Hurricanes coming into attack they immediately broke formation and scattered. Ray Holmes picked out one of the Dorniers to attack and his combat report tells what happened next:

> In the attack made by 504 Squadron, I attacked the right flank machine from quarter astern. Pieces flew from the wings and a flame appeared in the port wing, but

went out again. After breaking away I
climbed up to a single Dornier 215 and
made two quarter attacks. Pieces flew off.
My windscreen was now splashed with
black oil. I attacked a third time and a
member of the crew baled out. On my
fourth attack from the port beam, a jar
shook my starboard wing as I passed over
the enemy aircraft and I went into an
uncontrollable spin. I think the aircraft
must have exploded beneath me. I baled
out and as I landed, I saw the Dornier hit
the ground by Victoria Street Station half
a mile away.

Holmes had collided with the Dornier and part of his port
wing had been sliced off, the German aircraft had lost its
tail plane and its wingtips had separated in its plummeting
dive to earth. Holmes had managed to free himself from his
own stricken aircraft and his parachute had opened
successfully. His descent was a little worrying as he started
to drift towards the electric lines of the railway, but he
managed to veer his parachute away from this danger, but
was confronted with a three storey building. He hit the roof
and began to slide down the roof slates, suddenly he fell,
but his fall was stopped by a terrific jerk as his parachute
snagged and he was left hanging with his legs dangling in an
empty dustbin. He undid his parachute harness and
dropped to the ground and surveyed the situation. He had
landed in the back garden of the flats. He then noticed two
young girls who had appeared in the garden opposite and
greeted them both by kissing them on the cheek. He was
given use of a telephone and contacted his squadron back at
Hendon to tell them he was still alive and then was escorted
to Chelsea Barracks by a local Home Guard sergeant and
later returned by taxi to Hendon.

At just after midday, the Spitfires and Hurricanes of the
Duxford Wing engaged a large formation over Westerham,
Kent and severely mauled and shocked the Luftwaffe crews

as they were confronted not only by the usual small groups of fighters from 11 Group, but also a sixty strong wing from 12 Group. Leading the Duxford Wing was Squadron Leader Douglas Bader of No. 242 Squadron. Under his leadership the wing comprised of two Spitfire Squadrons, No. 19 and 611 the rest were Hurricanes of Nos 242, 310 Czech and 302 Polish Squadrons. They had assembled over Duxford, Cambridgeshire and proceeded south once news of the raids had developed. Bader was given orders to patrol south of the River Thames near Gravesend at 25,000 feet. At approximately 12.15, they sighted the enemy. In his combat report Bader wrote the following:

> I saw two squadrons pass underneath us in formation, travelling north-west in a purposeful manner, then saw anti-aircraft bursts, so turned 12 Group wing and saw enemy aircraft at 3,000 feet below to the north-west. Managed perfect approach with 19 and 611 between our Hurricanes and sun, and enemy aircraft below and down sun.
>
> Arrived over the enemy formation of 20-40 Dornier 17s and noticed 109s dive out of sun and warned Spitfires to look out. Me109 broke away and climbed south-east.
>
> About to attack enemy aircraft which was turning left handed, i.e. to west and south, when I noticed Spitfires and Hurricanes (11 Group?) engaging them. Was compelled to wait for risk of collision. However, warned wing to watch other friendly fighters and dived down with leading section in formation on to last section of three enemy aircraft. Pilot Officer Campbell took left hand Dornier 17; I took middle one and Sub Lieutenant

Cork the right hand one, which had lost ground on outside of turn.

Opened fire at 100 yards in a steep dive and saw a large flash behind the starboard motor of the Dornier as wing caught fire, must have hit petrol pipe or tank. I overshot and pulled up steeply then carried on and attacked another Dornier, but had to break away to avoid a Spitfire. The sky was full of Spitfires and Hurricanes queuing up and pushing each other out of the way to get at the Dorniers, which for once we outnumbered.

I squirted at odd Dorniers and closed range as they came into my sights, but could not hold them in my sights for fear of collision with other Spitfires and Hurricanes. I saw a <u>collision between a Spitfire and Dornier 17</u> which wrecked both aeroplanes. I finally ran out of ammunition chasing a crippled and smoking Dornier into cloud.

It was the finest shambles I have been in, since for once we had position, height and numbers. Enemy aircraft were a dirty looking collection.

(Had Bader witnessed the collision of Ray Homes Hurricane and the Dornier over central London?)

The German crews who had been mis-informed by their commanders that the Royal Air Force were now down to its last few remaining fighters; now had to contend with a stronger force of defenders. That morning's combat had sent the raiders fleeing back across the Channel with their tails firmly tucked between their legs.

As the deadly aerial ballet played out in the skies over London and the Kent countryside, at RAF Headquarters No. 11 Group, Uxbridge, Air-Vice Marshal Keith Park had suddenly been confronted by a surprise unannounced visit by the Prime Minister, Winston Churchill. What a time for such a visit? Churchill was given a seat in the balcony overlooking the large operations table below as WAAF plotters moved their information counters around the board, showing the position of incoming raids and RAF fighters now intercepting them. It was then that Churchill turned to Park and asked what reserve he had to fall back on. Park's famous reply was that there was none, all his squadrons had been thrown into the fight.

The next German assault came between 2.10 and 2.30 pm, when radar screens again showed aircraft formating over the Pas de Calais. The British fighter aircraft that had now been refuelled and re-armed were once more ordered to scramble into the air to intercept. In total twenty three squadrons from 11 Group, five from 12 Group and two from 10 Group had been ordered aloft. The Duxford Wing however did not gain the height necessary to take advantage over the German fighters and was in turn attacked as they climbed. The Wing was ordered to take evasive action and broke; it was every man for himself. A massive dogfight ensued.

As Spitfires turned and dived with their Messerschmitt opponents, the Hurricanes harried and shot down the bombers, which was far easier once they had lost their fighter cover. At 3.00 pm, Spitfires of No. 603 Squadron based at Hornchurch sighted a large Balbo of Heinkel 111s with fighter escort flying at 18,000 feet, 10 miles south of Chatham. Pilot Officer 'Ras' Berry of B Flight was one of those who engaged the formation, he later wrote:

> The squadron was patrolling at 22,000 feet, when I sighted a large number of fighters, 109s, above and several Vics of three of Heinkels below. The squadron went into line astern and peeled off on to the bombers. As I dived I saw a Messerschmitt attacking a Spitfire. I immediately split round and came on the 109s tail and at point blank range fired a

long burst. The 109 with heavy smoke pouring out went into a vertical dive into heavy cloud. Whilst patrolling around over Southend, I sighted a Dornier 17 homeward bound. A Hurricane and a Spitfire approached me and we all attacked the Dornier in turn. I gave a long burst on the enemy's starboard engine with success, but I had to break away with oil all over my windscreen from his aircraft. The enemy aircraft then glided down and pancaked in a field on the Isle of Sheppey. The crew of three climbed out and the aircraft began to burn slightly.

Flying Officer Eric Thomas of B Flight 222 Natal Squadron

On 15th September at approximately 2.15 pm I was patrolling with the squadron over Sheerness at 20,000 feet. Our formation had been broken up by enemy fighters; I dropped to 10,000 feet and noticed black anti-aircraft gunfire about ten miles away at about the same height in the direction of Chatham. By this time I was alone and saw a Dornier 17 flying alone heading due east. I disregarded the ack-ack fire and went into a beam attack out of the sun and managed to get in a short burst of fire at long range of 400-yards.

The enemy aircraft then disappeared into a cloud bank. I set my course due east and kept above the clouds and at about four miles further on, the Dornier appeared again. I did an astern attack and closed from 500 yards to 50 yards firing all the time. I saw pieces of aircraft flying off and the rear gun stopped firing. Just then a yellow nosed Bf109 appeared on my tail and I had to break off the attack and take cover in the cloud. Unfortunately the Dornier had disappeared by the time I came up again to look for it.

Flight Lieutenant 'Butch Barton 249 Squadron, North Weald:

We did everything to get at the enemy quickly. I had dived down from a considerable altitude to get at them and I had the speed. I latched onto a Messerschmitt 109, but at that same time he turned to fight and I had great difficulty in getting behind him again. Every time I closed up on him, he turned to fight. He climbed up into cloud and he thought he was going to be safe, it was just great that when I came out of the cloud that there he was, right out in front of me and that was his bad luck.

Flying Officer Peter Brown was flying with No. 611 Squadron and reflects on that momentous day:

I flew with the Duxford Wing and was involved in two battles over London. When we arrived with the Wing, we were the last and top squadron of the five-squadron Wing, which had three Hurricane squadrons followed by two Spitfire squadrons. There were so many aircraft in the sky, that the Germans were being attacked by numerous other British fighters; that we had to circle above waiting to get into battle. I felt at the time that there was something wrong with the control of our squadrons. In fact later reports show that sometimes there were two or even three British fighters queuing up to shoot down one German aircraft, whereas other formations were not attacked at all. The problem with the Bader Wing was that there was a heavily committed concentration of force that was not needed at that point.

I attacked a Dornier 215, which had previously been attacked by my commanding officer, Squadron Leader James McComb; but my front windscreen quickly became covered in oil from the damaged German that I had to break away. I then saw a Heinkel 111 on its own, and after I had opened fire, it went into a steep dive with the escape hatch over the cockpit open. I last saw it diving vertically to the ground and claimed it as a probable. Later I learned that two other pilots had also attacked this aircraft, which crashed, so the most I could claim was a third!

Sergeant George Unwin of 19 Squadron had his own view of the Duxford Big Wings' effectiveness that day:

The effect we had on the German pilots was tremendous. They had been told that the RAF hadn't really got many aircraft left now and it was going to be easier, then suddenly they came across sixty aircraft in one gaggle coming to meet them and it was very noticeable that the standard of their younger pilots was appalling.

The Messerschmitt fighters didn't need any excuse to go scuttling home. It was our job to keep the Messerschmitts away from our Hurricanes whose job it was to knock down the bombers. Douglas Bader who was leading the Wing and the Hurricane squadrons, were virtually unmolested, which was perfect, they could go back into the old Vic of three formation line astern, it really did work.

Hazel Gregory was working as a WAAF Plotter at the Operations Room at No.11 Group at Uxbridge on this day and recalls the events as they progressed

On 15th September, my watch took over in the Ops Room at 8.00 am to remain on duty until 4.00 pm. Before long it became clear that a massive daylight raid on London was taking place. Raids began showing up all over the plotting table. I plotted a very large formation of 400 aircraft coming in from the east and following the line of the Thames, heading straight for Westminster. Spitfires and Hurricanes from Debden, North Weald and Hornchurch were scrambled and from 12 Group to the north of our area, swept into attack. The enemy formations were broken up and we knew that dozens of individual battles were taking place over London.

Information from the RDF sites and the Observer Corps came in so fast that we were all concentrating to our utmost to carry out our duties calmly and efficiently at tremendous speed. At one stage we were visited by Mr. Churchill and a lady, who we later found out, was Mrs. Churchill talking to Air-Vice Marshal Park.

Height of Battle – 15th September 1940

From all the fighter stations in 11 Group and others, the lights on all the indicator panels in our Ops Room showed that every squadron was airborne. This was the time that Churchill turned to Keith Park and asked 'what reserves do we have' Park calmly replied 'None Sir.'

The battles raged all day and were beginning to ease off when we went off duty at 4.00 pm. We had our evening meal and a rest and went back on duty at midnight for the night shift. Things were quiet by then. In the small hours an NCO came in to chalk up the boards headed 'Enemy aircraft destroyed' and 'RAF aircraft lost.' The figures were stunning, 185 Germans destroyed and only 27 RAF lost. I knew that later the actual figure was a lot fewer.

Fighter Command Operational Report from 12.30 p.m. to 6.00 p.m. 15th September 1940.

General

During the period there were two major attacks on London, in which 500 or more enemy aircraft appeared to have been engaged. Preliminary reports indicate the fighter escorts were small in comparison with the number of bombers. 12 Group operated 5 Squadrons as a wing on each occasion, with Spitfires at 26,000 feet attacking fighters, and Hurricanes at 25,000 feet attacking bombers.

The enemy fighters did not defend the bomber formations when attacked and left both Spitfires and Hurricanes to attack the bombers; 43 enemy aircraft were destroyed and 3 of our fighters were lost. One twin-engine enemy aircraft was reported with Italian markings. There were also attacks in the afternoon on Portland and Southampton.

Height of Battle – 15th September 1940

<u>First attack on London 12.30 - 12.45 hours</u>
This attack was preceded by extensive enemy patrols in the Straits of Dover between 10.00 and 11.00 hours, and two flights over Dover and Ramsgate about 10.40 hours.

At 11.33 hours a large formation of enemy aircraft crossed the coast between Dover and Folkestone and was followed within the next three minutes by two further formations which flew in over Dover and the South Foreland. All three raids took a zig-zag course to start with, flying first in a northerly direction as if they were all going straight out over north east Kent and the Thames Estuary. They all, however, turned south or south west before reaching the north coast of Kent and out, flying on over the whole of the London area.

The attack was broken up before 12.30 hours, and most of the surviving enemy aircraft re-crossed the coast at various points between Beachy Head and the north Foreland, the remainder returning over the Thames Estuary. Probably 200 or more enemy aircraft were engaged in this attack, the objectives of which appeared to have been Gas Works and industrial targets in the London area and possibly also the docks and aerodromes around London.

Bombs were dropped on the Crystal Palace, Clapham Common, Anerley, Norbury, Upper Tooting, Wandsworth, Kensington, Thornton Heath, Battersea and Chelsea areas.
To meet this attack, 20 Squadrons were sent up from 11 Group, 5 from 12 Group, and 1 from 10 Group.

<u>Second Attack on London 13.45 – 15.30 hours</u>
The first attack had hardly been dispersed before enemy aircraft again began to mass in the Calais-Boulogne area for a further attack. Between 14.10 and 14.34 hours, eight or more formations of enemy aircraft crossed the coast between Rye and Dover and headed for London.
Probably 300 or more enemy aircraft were engaged in this attack, the objectives of which appeared to have been similar to those of the first attack, but a small proportion of the enemy aircraft got through to the London area.

Height of Battle – 15th September 1940

Bombs were dropped on Woolwich, Barking, Stepney, Hackney Marshes, Stratford Gasworks, West Ham, Penge and a Petrol Depot at West Ham Park. The enemy aircraft re-crossed the coast over a wide area, at points between Beachy Head and the North Foreland.

To meet this attack, 23 Squadrons were sent up from 11 Group, 5 from 12 Group and 3 from 10 Group.

Attack on Portland 14.35 hours
About 25 enemy aircraft from the Cherbourg area flew in over and bombed Portland, going on at once east over St. Albans Head, and then South East in the direction of Cherbourg.

Attack on Southampton Area 17.45 – 18.15 hours
About 40 enemy aircraft from the Cherbourg area flew in from the Isle of Wight and made for Southampton, but turned almost immediately and flew back on this course after dropping about 24 bombs around Marchwood and in the Hamble district.

Reconnaissances
Patrols in the Straits of Dover and flights over the east coast of Kent before 11.00 hours.

Flights over (1) Lyme Bay, Middle Wallop, Oxford, Bristol Channel and South Cerney, and (2) Manchester, Liverpool, Wales and the Bristol Channel.

Weather
Weather was mainly fair or fine at first with good visibility becoming fair to cloudy during the morning with some showers mainly in the north and west and with cloud at 2,000 feet to 3,000 feet lowering to 1,000 to 2,000 feet and showers.

Height of Battle – 15th September 1940

A.A. Guns in Action

Dover	10.44 hours	20,000 ft.	Target 1 He.111.
Dover	1131-1154	12,000-18,000 ft.	Target 20+ Do.17's 20+ Me.109's
Dover	1415-1644	1,500-9,000 ft.	
Crewe	1143-1145	20,000 ft.	Target 1 Ju.88
Mersey	1149	12,000 ft.	
		19,000 ft.	
I.A.Z	1157-1215	14,000-21,000 ft	
	1429-1430	16,000-17,000 ft.	
Thames & Medway	1211 hours	27,000 ft.	Target 3 Me.109's
	1430	22,000 ft.	3 Me.109's
	1433	19,000 ft.	3 He.111's
Thames & Medway.	1200 hours	14,000 ft.	10 Me.109's
S			20 He.111's
Portland	1531-1532	16,000 ft.	
Southampton	1752-1758	8,000-12,000 ft.	

As the retreating German Air Force headed back to France during the late afternoon, the pilots of Fighter Command realised that they had dealt a serious blow against the enemy and their plans for invasion. Initial reports for that day claimed that 185 German aircraft had been destroyed. This was an incredible moral boost for the nation, especially for the people living in the East End of London, who had suffered much during the last several days of bombing. Sadly the figures in reality were much less. Later records would confirm that only fifty-six enemy aircraft had been destroyed for the loss of twenty-seven aircraft of Fighter Command.

Over the next two days, the weather turned unfavourable with cloud and rain during the day, but during the night, the Germans were able to launch attacks and bombed London, Bristol and Merseyside.

CHAPTER 10

You Never See the One that
Shoots You Down!

Air combat has always been envisaged by those viewing on the ground as a dramatic duel between two equals, whose skill would depend on the most talented in the final outcome. During the Battle of Britain and throughout the war, most combats were quick, deadly affairs, the advantage obtained by those with height, speed and mostly attacking their targets, whom had been totally oblivious to the threat that was seconds away.

The famous scenes of dogfights lasting minutes were more likely to be counted in seconds as pilots fired short bursts of machine gun at fleeting aircraft that twisted and turned in the fourth dimension.

The pilot that had the advantage of height and surprise over his opponent could direct his attack and control the battle. If attacking bomber formations this was of great importance, thus giving a short time to decide at what angle to best approach without suffering to much damage to ones self. But once committed to the attack, this then left one open to the German fighter escorts, which more than likely would be hovering over their charges like bees guarding a hive.

In the maelstrom that becomes air combat; many a young fighter pilot would never see the aircraft that shot him down. Once totally immersed in the fight for survival at speeds sometimes in access of 400 mph, pilots were killed not knowing what had hit them. Fortunately, some pilots did survive, either baling out or being able to return to base in badly shot up aircraft and alive to tell the tale.

Here are some of those who recall their dramatic and frightening experiences. Sergeant Pilot Denis Robinson was to experience such event against the German opposition while flying with No.152 Squadron based at RAF Warmwell, they covered the south-west of England.

175

You never see the one that shoots you down!

I was shot down on 8th August 1940. By this time I had already claimed a 109 destroyed on 25th July and another on 5th August; but now it was my turn to be shot down by Bf109s of II/JG53 off Swanage in Dorset.

The facts are not particularly gratifying for either myself or Pilot Officer Stephen Beaumont, who was also shot down with me that day. We were returning from a patrol in which we had intercepted the enemy and had used all our ammunition. Our eight Browning machine guns used ammo fast due to the limited space in the Spitfires wings, and there was never more than 15-seconds total fire power available. So we were returning to our base at Warmwell to refuel and re-arm.

There were three of us flying in Vic formation, with Beaumont on the left of the flight leader and myself on the right. We were flying in a very tight formation, probably about a couple of fight from the leaders wingtips. Therefore both Beaumont and I had our eyes and concentration fixed clearly on the leaders' aircraft. This was the way that we flew in close formation early in the battle, until we learnt better later.

Unfortunately, a group of Bf109s spotted us and carried out an attack on our unprotected rear, which we offered to them on a plate. We ought to have known better. We all knew that is was vital to keep a good lookout at all times, but we were lulled into a false sense of security and had relaxed our vigilance briefly; after all, we had had our scrap, were nearly

176

You never see the one that shoots you down!

safely home and anyway, we had no ammunition.

The first thing I felt was the thud of bullets hitting my aircraft and a long line of tracer bullets streaming out ahead of my Spitfire. In a reflex action, I slammed the stick forward as far as it would go. For a brief second my aircraft stood on its nose and I was looking down at Mother Earth, thousands of feet below. Thank God my Sutton harness was good and tight. I could feel the straps biting into my flesh as I entered the vertical with airspeed building up alarmingly. I felt fear mounting. Sweating, mouth dry and near panic. No ammo and an attacker right on my tail.

All this happened in seconds, now the airspeed was nearly off the clock. I simply had to pull out and start looking for the enemy. That's what I did, turning and climbing at the same time. As I opened up the throttle fully, with emergency boost selected to assist the climb, I noticed wisps of white smoke coming from the nose of my Spitfire. God, no! Fire! Suddenly the engine stopped. Apparently a bullet had hit my glycol tank and had dispersed all the coolant; even my faithful Merlin engine could not stand that for long. That's what had caused the white smoke.

The dread of being burnt to death was one of the worst fears. It drew heavily on any reserves of courage one had. The release of tension as I realised my good fortune is something that cannot be described. You only know what it is like

You never see the one that shoots you down!

to be given back your life, if you have been through that experience.

I still had plenty of height and time to think. I prepared to bale out and began going through the procedure in my mind. While I was preparing, I had got the aircraft into a steady glide, it was still flying reasonably well and the controls still responsive. I could see no damage accept for a few bullet holes here and there on my starboard wing. It then began to worry me that if I abandoned the Spitfire, it my crash onto a house or God knows what and cause other casualties. So I decided to try and make a forced-landing in a field, if I could find one suitable. Most of the fields looked pretty small, so I decided it would be landing with the wheels up.

I picked a field near Wareham that looked suitable, slid back the canopy and commenced an approach. At 200 feet, the boundary loomed up. I gave it full flap and achieved a creditable touchdown. So far so good, I thought as the Spitfire slithered along the grass. Suddenly, I felt the aircraft go up on her nose and then with an almighty crash the canopy hood slammed shut over my head, filled with dirt which almost blinded me.

The Spitfire seemed to have turned upside down and I wondered whether I was now trapped. I grabbed the canopy lever and it opened immediately, thank goodness.   To my amazement, the aircraft was standing on its nose in a ditch. I jumped from the cockpit and stood there surveying the scene as local people arrived to look at the aircraft and then

You never see the one that
shoots you down!

whisked me off to the local pub in nearby Wareham and proceeded to give me glasses full of spirit. I had a slight bullet graze on my leg, but I was otherwise unhurt. Next day I was back on operations again.

Sergeant Pilot Bill Green was just 19 and serving with 501 Squadron based at Gravesend. On 28th August, he was scrambled along with the rest of 'B' Flight to patrol at 12,000 feet over Deal. He remembers what took place next:

We received information from the controller on the ground and our commanding officer Squadron Leader Hogan led us up to look for a formation at 'Angels Twenty'. The next thing I recall happening was the crash of glass made by a bullet smashing through my so-called bullet proof windscreen in front about the size of a tennis ball; I then felt glycol streaming over me, giving me a shower. The radiator return pipe was hit as it was cool glycol not steaming hot, luckily for me.

I had been wounded in the knee by shell splinters and I decided there and then it was time to vacate my aircraft. I jumped and pulled the chute, but it didn't deploy properly and wrapped around me like a roller towel. I dropped from 17,000 feet down to 500 feet before it opened. Very lucky to survive, I was picked up in a field in the Eltham Valley and then taken to the Woolwich General Hospital for treatment. I never saw the chap who shot me down. One minute everything was OK, the next I was fighting to stay alive.

You never see the one that
shoots you down!

Sergeant Len Davies of 151 Squadron was another who was shot down on the same day as Bill Green; and had to deal with the frightening realities of being shot at unexpectedly from an unknown enemy. In seconds, he was from one moment flying along happily, then having to fight to control his aircraft and stay alive.

When I took off for the last time on 28th August, the Germans were bombing the airfield, When it all started I was doing the job of arse-end Charlie, watching the tails of the squadron, keeping an eye out for any enemy attack. When we got the order to go in line astern and dived like mad. I was left a little behind because of my job, but when we got into the fight it was mainly Messerschmitt 109s and it was a complete shambles with aircraft crossing all over the sky. I just pressed the firing button if one flew across in front of me.

I was rejoining the formation afterwards and received a message over the radio from Flight Lieutenant Irving Smith and I was throttling back alongside him virtually, when I was hit. I only knew I had been hit when I heard a cannon shell explode inside my cockpit, I then got the hell out of it and quickly manoeuvred my aircraft down. I had been wounded in the leg from the attack and was leaking quite a bit. I sighted Eastchurch, but when I crash-landed they had just been bombing the runways there. I managed to get down, but it was all very dicey.

Unfortunately I had lost a lot of blood by then, I managed successfully to landed my damaged Hurricane, but it cart-wheeled over in a bomb crater I hadn't

You never see the one that shoots you down!

seen and I was left hanging upside down in my straps. I then passed out. I was then carefully removed from the cockpit and the medics stripped me off in the air-raid shelter and was given first aid on my leg, there was blood everywhere, which probably made it look a lot worse than it was, I had also hit my forehead on the gun-sight and this left me with a small hole in my forehead, which I still have today. At the hospital they fished out all the metal splinters in my leg and it was annoying that it took a while to heal. It was well into November before I got home on leave. By the time I returned to the squadron, they were then converting to night fighters.

Flight Lieutenant 'Butch' Barton had been intercepted a enemy formation with 249 Squadron on September 5th, when he was clobbered from an unknown source:

Just when you think you are going to get one, suddenly out of nowhere you get hit, that's a very nasty thing. You think to yourself 'Hell, that's bad, the damn things now on fire, what a disappointment. How do I get out of this damn thing? A I fell through the sky I said 'Well now you better open the parachute, you'd better find the ripcord which is located on your chest' all the while I was falling through the sky. The chute opened and when I finally landed I crashed through and stripped a Pear tree down in somebody's backyard, fortunately I was unhurt except for a few bruises and light cuts.

You never see the one that
shoots you down!

Pilot Officer Gerald Stapleton of 603 'City of Edinburgh' Squadron had been in action during the latter part of the afternoon of 7th September, he recalls the following event:

> I never saw the guy that brought me down, we had been in action and were reforming just north of London; we didn't have any rearguard aircraft weaving behind us keeping a look out, when suddenly my aircraft was hit by cannon shells. One of the shells exploded between the second and third machine guns on my starboard wing and laid them open; I could see the ammunition feeds trailing over the wing. I had no aileron control and as soon as I opened up the engine throttle, the glycol fumes came into my cockpit. I instantly opened my cockpit hood. I then tried to fly as straight as I could until I saw a stubble field, which I aimed for to land. I did a flat turn on the rudder and overshot the stubble field and landed in a hop field next door. I had my wheels up and I torpedoed across the field about two feet off the ground. Once the aircraft was stationary I got out and noticed a country lane close by. There I noticed a family having a picnic and they offered me a cup of tea, which I gratefully accepted. I was then given a lift in their Austin Ruby saloon.

Flying Officer Harold 'Birdie' Wilson was flying with 17 Squadron operating from Debden in Essex. On 27th September, he and his comrades had been scrambled to intercept a formation of bombers; he remembers what happened to him on that fateful day:

182

You never see the one that shoots you down!

We saw the bombers ahead of us, we had been scrambled a bit late and we were at a height of between 15,000 to 16,000 feet chasing the bombers really. Then suddenly just south of the Thames area, Spitfires came diving down through our formation and we were a bit worried about that. We didn't realise that they were being chased by 109s and the next thing I experienced was a terrific bang in the cockpit and flames coming up from my fuel tank. I looked up and found I had no Perspex left in my hood and it was getting fairly hot, so I decided I better get out. I baled out immediately and I noticed the quietness after baling out.

The battle was going on, I could hear the rat a tat tat of guns going off in the distance and also the noise of engines from fellow pilots in the squadron, circling round to make sure one got down safely. I was slightly wounded with shrapnel and stuff and as I floated down it was very peaceful; as I looked down I could see a naval torpedo boat coming out to intercept me in the mouth of the Thames and this they did.

It was some forty-two years later in 1982, that I found out that I had been shot down by the German ace Adolf Galland and that day I had been his fortieth victim. This had won him the Knight of the Iron Cross. I wrote to him and told him I had been the sucker he had shot down.

You never see the one that
shoots you down!

Bird-Wilson was taken from the naval vessel and on landing was admitted to the Royal Naval Hospital at Chatham. He returned to his squadron a week later.

Sergeant Reg Gretton of 222 Natal Squadron remembers his experience of being bounced by unseen enemy fighters over Maidstone on 27th September.

It was another of those occasions when the sky had cleared of aircraft. I had looked all around and hadn't spotted anything, when suddenly I was hit; whoever it was had got my glycol tank. Once the glycol started streaming out, I just switched off the engine and dived down. I undid my Sutton harness straps and pulled back the canopy ready to bale-out.

When I was down to about 5,000 feet, I realised that the engine was not going to catch fire. The Spitfire was not flying very well and by the time I was down to 100 feet, ready to crash-land, I realised that I had not re-tightened my Sutton harness. The aircraft stalled at about ten feet and smacked into the ground. I'd turned off the switches and the petrol, so there was no fire. As the aircraft slurried along the ground, I hit my head on the gun-sight and passed out. I had also badly damaged my back and pelvis. I remember being lifted on to the wing by my rescuers and then was rushed off to Oldchurch Hospital in Romford.

I spent the following five months recovering from a fractured pelvis and spine. It was not until June 1941, before I was posted to the Aircraft Delivery Flight at Hendon to resume flying.

You never see the one that shoots you down!

On the same day Sergeant 'Wag' Haw of 504 Squadron had been engaged in combat over Bristol and relates the following:

If you talk to pilots who have been shot down, nearly half of them will tell you they never would have been, if they had seen it coming. I didn't see what shot me down although there were lots of aircraft in the sky at that time. I had already shot one down myself, a Messerschmitt 110 and suddenly I was looking for someone else, then instantly there was a smell of burning, something had hit the oil tank and then the engine seized up. The engine was useless and there were lots of aeroplanes about. There was our squadron and about forty Me110s and I thought the best thing I can do is make it look like I've had it, so I put my aircraft into a spin at about 10 to 12,000 feet and kept it in this spin until I was sure that I was clear of any danger. I pulled out and then put the flaps down and landed in a field wheels up.

There was a chap who had been doing his farm work and he was quite cross about it, he didn't know if I was English or not, but I hastily made myself known and with my parachute slung over my shoulder and walked to the road nearby, where there was a chap who I think was a commercial traveler, he gave me a lift to the nearest pub where I could use a telephone. I tried to get through, but all the lines to Bristol were down due to the bombing, so I couldn't tell anyone where I

You never see the one that
shoots you down!

was. I eventually got back at 11.30 that
evening after being shot down at 10.00
that morning.

He force-landed his Hurricane P3415 at Gammons Farm,
Kilmington, Axeminster, he had been shot down by
Oberleutnant Roedel of 4/JG27, who claimed a Hurricane
in that area.

Pilot Officer Richard Jones had fought with 64 Squadron
during the early part of the battle and now had been posted
to No.19 Squadron on 20th September 1940. On the 28th
of that month his squadron had been ordered to patrol
between London and Kent. He clearly remembers the
following sequence of events:

We had a message come over the R/T
that no enemy aircraft were in our vicinity
and we were ordered back to base. I was
flying as arse-end Charlie, so I relaxed and
the next thing I looked over to my
starboard wing to see a bloody great hole
had appeared in it. Then there was a large
bang and I suddenly realised that I had
been shot at, but there was no sign of an
enemy aircraft anywhere. I never saw an
aircraft nor later did anybody else in our
formation. The squadron carried on home
to base completely unaware that I was
missing and that I had been hit by enemy
fire and was heading down with a
damaged Spitfire.

My engine cut out and I stalled at 160
mph instead of 100 and went into a spin.
It didn't come out of the spin from 20,000
feet until I was down to about 10,000 feet,
I hadn't enough movement with the
controls, but I eventual got it under
control and it was over Hawkhurst that I

You never see the one that shoots you down!

spotted two suitable fields for putting the aircraft down. They were bare, the only two in a much wooded area. I aimed for the first, but missed it and hit the second on crash-landing, landed on some sheep, a hell of a bloody mess I can assure you. I was alright, accept for a wound to my leg, the plane received minor damage from the landing and the farm labourers who were bringing in the harvest; they came over with their pitch-forks thinking I was a German.

The army eventually came along and picked me up and took me to their mess nearby, gave me lunch and said 'now you can take off your flying suit off' I said 'I can't I've only got my pyjamas on underneath.' I returned back to Fowlmere and was operational again the next day. Such was life at this time. If you had to fly three or four times a day, you would be tired out, but you did it.

In my logbook I wrote, Shot down and crash-landed at Hawkhurst, Kent. Killed three sheep. What a bloody mess!

Ben Bennions was a seasoned and experienced fighter pilot, having served in the RAF since the late 1920s. He had served with No. 41 Squadron for many years and was respected for his knowledge and leadership of tactics and gunnery; but even this would not prepare him for the following action that took place in the skies over southern England on 1st October 1940:

As far as I was concerned it was just a normal patrol, and I was at about 28,000 feet, I haven't a clue really what happened, just that suddenly there was a crash bang

You never see the one that
shoots you down!

wallop and I was out. How I got out I don't know, I think it must have been an automatic reaction. I can't even remember getting out of the aeroplane.

All I can remember is breathing a sigh of relief when I pulled the ripcord, I couldn't use my right hand and I was pushing and pulling with the left hand and finally the chute opened, I then passed out. I don't remember hitting the ground.

When I landed in the field some people brought me to a farmhouse, and the farmer's wife, she said 'bring him into the kitchen' and they said, 'Oh no, it's not worth it, he won't last that long' so they left me outside and sent for the ambulance. I was taken to Horsham base hospital first, I don't think that's far from East Grinstead, I was taken there and seen by the plastic surgeon Archibald MacIndoe, because I had lost my left eye. A cannon shell had exploded in my face and injured the left side; I was also wounded in my right arm and my right leg.

The farmer did write to me afterwards as he was ex-RAF bloke and told me roughly what had happened. Apparently one of the locals that had helped to pick me up christened a racehorse that had been born soon after and named it 'Bennions Spitfire'.

At East Grinstead they patched me up, did quite a bit of plastic surgery, they got my right hand working again, my legs tidied up a little.

MacIndoe was a wonderful man as was all the staff that worked there. There were

Aircraftswoman Avis Hearn was a radar operator at the Chain Home RDF Station at Poling when it was attacked on 18th August by Stukas. Avis remained at her post continuing to send information to RAF Headquarters at Stanmore and was later awarded the Military Medal for her courage under fire. (Courtesy of Chesham Museum)

Alan Deere from New Zealand. He became an ace and was shot down twice and his air craft blown up on take-off during an enemy raid. He died in 1995 (Authors Collection)

RDF Chain Home Airmen & WAAF operators at work in the Receiver hut at Ventnor, Isle of Wight. (Copyright IWM C1868)

A flight of Hawker Hurricane Mk 1s of No. 151 Squadron take to the air on a patrol from North Weald aerodrome. On the ground, Hurricane aircraft of 56 Squadron are seen taxiing into position. In the background can be seen the radio wireless masts at Weald Gullet. (Copyright IWM CH 162)

Boulton-Paul Defiant fighters of No. 264 Squadron. This aircraft had a performance not dissimilar to that of a Spitfire or Hurricane, but due to the weight of the turret and the added disadvantage of not having forward wing mounted machine guns, the German fighters soon had the measure of this aircraft. As casualties mounted at an alarming rate, the Defiant was withdrawn from the battle and used as a night-fighter. (Copyright IWM CH 884)

Sergeant Bill Green of 501 Squadron seated in his Hurricane whilst operating from Gravesend aerodrome.

(Courtesy of F/Lt William Green)

Pilot Officers' Crelin 'Bogle' Bodie and John 'Durex' Kendal of No.66 Squadron take time out to relax at Gravesend aerodrome. Sadly neither survived the war.

(Courtesy of Military Trader.co.uk)

The wrecked Hurricane fighter P3320 in which Sergeant Len Davies crash-landed after being shot down on 28th August 1940, the aircraft was repaired by the No.1 Civilian Repair Unit at Crowley, Oxfordshire and flew again.

(Courtesy of Len Davies)

Sergeant Joan Mortimer, Flight Officer Elspeth Henderson and Sergeant Helen Turner seen outside one of the damaged buildings at Biggin Hill aerodrome after the heavy attacks on 31st August & 1st September. All three WAAF's were awarded the Military Medal for their courage and devotion to duty during the raids. (Copyright IWM CH1550)

An aerial photograph of North Weald aerodrome, following the attacks made by the Luftwaffe in August and September. Note the bomb craters dotted around the perimeter track as well as the main flight paths. (Courtesy of North Weald Airfield Museum)

A Spitfire of No. 222 Natal Squadron stands ready for its next flight at Hornchurch in September 1940. This particular aircraft was flown by the squadrons' commanding officer Squadron Leader Johnny Hill. A Bristol Blenheim of 600 Squadron can also be seen in the background. (Copyright of Mr Joe Crawshaw)

A Heinkel He111 bomber being prepared by ground-crew for another sortie over England during the summer of 1940. (Authors Collection)

This evocative photograph of aircraft contrails shows the passage of battle high over central London and Parliament in September 1940. (Crown Copyright 122823)

A photograph taken from a gun-camera from the Spitfire of Squadron Leader H.S Darley of 609 Squadron shows the moment he opens fire on a Heinkel He111 of KG55, following the attack on the Supermarine aircraft works at Woolston, Southampton. (Copyright IWM CH 1829)

John Burgess flew Spitfires and served with No.222 Natal Squadron based at RAF Hornchurch and Rochford throughout the battle.

(Authors collection courtesy of Neil Burgess)

Safe return to Hornchurch. Flying Officer John 'Mac' Mackenzie steps down from his No.41 Squadron Spitfire following combat in October 1940.
(Authors Collection)

Flying Officer Peter Brown of 41 Squadron returns from another sortie. Pictured with Peter are the Adjutant, Flying Officer Stevens and Squadron Leader Don Finlay who pre-war was an Olympic hurdler. (Authors Collection)

A Luftwaffe bomber crew go over their flight plans for their next mission over England. (Authors Collection)

A symbol of defiance! St. Paul's Cathedral stands out amongst the smoke & flames of burning London, after another succession of attacks by the Luftwaffe. (Copyright IWM HU 36220)

Flying Officer Tom Neil of No. 249 Squadron based at North Weald. He went on to become an ace pilot and later flew in the defence of Malta. (Copyright IWM CH 2750)

Iain Hutchinson flew with 222 Squadron as a sergeant pilot based at Hornchurch. He was shot down twice and survived to become a senior experimental officer for the Atomic Energy Authority during the 1950s. (Authors Collection)

F/Lt Brian Kingcome led 92 Squadron many times into combat from Biggin Hill in 1940. He later served out in the Mediterranean during the invasion of Sicily & Italy and was promoted to group captain. He died in 1994. (Copyright IWM CH 3553)

South African Gerald 'Stapme' Stapleton of 603 'City of Edinburgh Squadron, was one of many young pilots who came from the Commonwealth, joined the RAF and fought during the battle. (Copyright of Davis M. Ross)

Life goes on? The wedding of Ronald 'Wally' Wallens who served with No. 41 Squadron during the battle. Other Battle of Britain pilots identified who attended the ceremony are from left to right: front Jackie Mann, 3rd Reginald Gretton, 7th Ivor Cosby and far right Arthur Spears. (Courtesy of Mrs M. Spears)

You never see the one that shoots you down!

other pilots there I remember, Geoffrey Page was in Ward 3. I went over to his ward, not to see him, but another chap whom I had been friends with at school, his name was Ralph Carnell, he was a Hurricane pilot. He was bed ridden because his wounds were in both legs. When I staggered into Ward 3, I was absolutely horrified; I'd never seen anything like it. One chap came along with no lips just teeth showing, no eyebrows, bulging eyes and he came along and picked up a chair with his mouth and slung it along the floor and said 'Have a seat old boy.' After seeing this, what did I have to complain about? Then I went back again, I was there about two or three months. They let me home for Christmas, then I went back again; I was there about two or three months.

Brian Kingcome of No. 92 Squadron was a seasoned veteran pilot having flown in the RAF since 1938. He had gained much experience during the early battles over Dunkirk and was now a flight commander. His experience of being shot down was that he was possibly a victim of friendly fire, although this was never proved:

We had been engaged over Maidstone what was then towards the end of the Battle of Britain and to sound a bit blasé it was becoming a bit of a routine. We did the usual thing, engaged and fired our ammunition and then the usual thing happened that every World War two pilot will confirm, the sky was suddenly empty of aeroplanes. I had fired all my ammunition, looked round and there was

189

You never see the one that shoots you down!

nothing about, it was a beautiful day and nothing in the sky except three Spitfires behind me.

I saw Biggin Hill in the distance and did the most stupid of things; I decided to practice a forced landing, so I throttled back and started to glide towards Biggin from about 20,000 feet which was visible in the distance. All of a sudden there was a rat tat tat and my aircraft was full of bullets and my leg was hit, and I though 'Jesus' and I looked round and alongside me came three Spitfires. They took one look at me and half rolled away. Now, whether they shot someone off my tail or whether they had a quick burst before they realised their mistake, I just don't know.

Looking down at my leg that had been hit, I saw blood beginning to flow over the top of my flying boot, which was somewhat disconcerting. I was left deciding my next course of action, either to stay with the aircraft and hopefully bring her into land, with the hope of no other structural failings or to bale out before passing out due to loss of blood. I decided the latter. I baled out and hoped that the parachute was not damaged in any way. Floating down over the Kent countryside, I landed heavily on mother earth and rolled over with my breath knocked out of me.

Nearby were a couple of farm workers who attended me and transported me to Chatham Hospital. A surgeon worked on my leg and patched it up and the next morning I was then transferred to

You never see the one that shoots you down!

Orpington Hospital to have the bullet removed. I was out of action for about six weeks before returning to active duty.

CHAPTER 11

The Tide has Turned

Following the large raids and the dramatic shock that the Luftwaffe aircrews had suffered when confronted by the 12 Group Big Wing formations on 15th September, showed that the Royal Air Force was far from beaten. The next few days were not as hectic, on 16th and 17th the weather changed again and was deemed unsuitable to carry out large raids; instead the Germans carried out large fighter sweeps escorting small formations of bombers. The old tactic of trying to lure the RAF was once more brought into effect.

Luftwaffe formations crossed the coast between Deal and Lympne on 16th, but were intercepted early by British fighters and following running clashes with the main enemy force, the raiders only got as far as Maidstone. There was no way of stopping the night-bombers who again returned that evening to bomb the capital unhindered apart from the anti-aircraft defences. The only RAF success that night was the bringing down of a Junkers Ju88 of 1/KG54, which crashed at St.Andrew's Close, Maidstone just before midnight, shot down by a Defiant night-fighter of 141 Squadron.

It was not only the Luftwaffe that had been busy that night. Plans to bomb German invasion barges sitting ready in ports along the French coast had been undertaken from as early as the 7th September and were put into effect by squadrons of Bomber Command.

While Fighter Command was battling to keep the Luftwaffe at bay by day, the little known facts do not highlight the role played by Bomber and Coastal Command during that summer. From 13th to 20th September, 618 sorties were carried out. The 17th September saw raids against the ports at Calais, Boulogne, Cherbourg and further north at den Helder in the Netherlands. Many barges and naval vessels were badly damaged and ammunition stores were destroyed.

The Tide has Turned

It was on this day that Luftwaffe, Kriegsmarine and Wehrmacht commanders along the coast of France received the news that Hitler in Berlin had decided to postpone 'Operation Sealion' indefinitely.
The following document stated:

OKW   Berlin 17 Sep 1940

After consultation with group commanders of the armed forces, the Führer has reached the following decisions:

1. 'Seelöwe'

    (a) The commencement of the operation will be further postponed. A new order (gem. OKW Sec 1 No. 33255/40
Corps HQ of 3.9.40 fig2) will be issued on 17.9.40
All preparations will be continued.

    (b) Neutralisation of English long range batteries firing on the
French coast will be carried out by the Air Force as soon as preparations for this purpose are completed.

    (c) In this situation it will not be necessary yet to carry into
effect over the complete area the special measures provided for in the coastal services.
(OKW No. 2552/40 Corps HQ Security IIIc of 29.8.40)
On the other hand, the necessary security and counter espionage measures will be tightened up within a framework to be defined between the Army GHQ (Security) and Naval GHQ and the Cs-in-C for the individual coastal sectors.

The Tide has Turned

2. <u>Air attacks on London</u>

Air attacks on London will be carried out over wider areas than hitherto, indeed from now on will be aimed definitely on targets important from a military point of view and those vital to the life of the great city (including the Railway stations). These will continue until there are no more such targets to be neutralised.

Terror attacks against purely residential quarters will continue to be the last resort and therefore will not yet be carried out.

C-in-C Armed Forces,
Keitel

This document states that attacks against the British civilian population was a last resort, Hitler himself had given a speech on 4th September at the Sportsplast calling for the raising of British cities to the ground after RAF Bomber Command had retaliated and bombed Berlin.

Fine weather returned once more on the 18th and the Luftwaffe launched large raids again that morning. At 9.27 am 150 aircraft were picked up by radar heading in towards the Kent coast. On the way in towards London, one formation separated and bombed Chatham dockyard. The other formations reached London where they were harassed on the way in and out back over Kent.

A second raid came in at around 12.35 pm with 150 aircraft of Luftflotte 2 forming into two large formations. Heading up the Thames Estuary towards London, they were intercepted by squadrons from 11 Group and individual combats ensued between fighter versus fighter as well as against bombers. The final attack against London came at around 4.00 pm, when 100 aircraft crossed the coast of east Kent, but this was repulsed by RAF fighters in running battles.

The Duxford Wing claimed 29 aircraft destroyed that afternoon, but in reality the figures show that only four

The Tide has Turned

Junker Ju88s were brought down; two each shot down by 19 Squadron and 302 Polish Squadron. The final tally to both sides that day was 12 RAF fighters lost with nine pilots safe against 33 Luftwaffe destroyed.

John Burgess of 222 Squadron remembers there seemed to be more new aggressive spirit and vigor after the 15th September amongst our own men and that the German fighters seemed less likely to want to mix it with the Spitfires:

> One of the things that really put things in perspective as far as I was concerned, was that one day in the middle of September 1940, over southern England, I was returning to base after the squadron had been in an engagement. Suddenly looking into my rear view mirror two aircraft appeared, they were 109s travelling fast up behind me. So I pulled up into a steep climb to meet them head on, as soon as I did this they both rolled on to their backs, turned tail and ran. They had had me at a complete disadvantage and could have shot me down as easy as pie, but as soon as I made an aggressive move towards them, they just turned and ran. You realise then that they are just as frightened as you are, possibly more so. It gives you a certain feeling of superiority, a slight smugness perhaps, better than they are. You were frightened on many occasions, not normally when you're involved in an engagement with a 109, where you are too busy to be frightened.

The next day, 19th September saw very little enemy air activity with only single German reconnaissance aircraft venturing over the Channel, the Liverpool area and South Wales. The 20th September saw small raids against London

The Tide has Turned

during the morning, but these were mainly fighter sweeps, getting only as far as Hornchurch before turning back at 11.35 pm. There were no further raids that day. One RAF pilot who intercepted the raid on its return back to France was Flying Officer Eric Thomas of 222 Squadron based at Hornchurch. He stated in his report:

> I was climbing to patrol with five aircraft, when at 25,000 feet; a squadron of yellow-nosed 109 fighters attacked us from the sun in a quarter attack. I saw tracer shells going past Pilot Officer Edsall and I broke away and got on the tail of the 109. I opened fire from astern at approximately 200 yards and gave two long bursts of five seconds. I saw trails of white vapour then come away from the enemy aircraft.
>
> I broke away and carried out a deflection attack on two more 109s circling round in tight formation, but saw no result, as I had to break away, as I was then attacked myself.

The next large bomber attack did not materialize until Tuesday 24th September, at 8.30 that morning radar picked up 200 aircraft crossing the Channel in five formations at altitudes of between 10,000 to 15,000 feet and covering a ten mile front between Dover and Dungeness. Bombs were dropped on installations at Gravesend and Tilbury on the Thames Estuary, before they turned for home. A second raid of 100 aircraft came in over the Dover area at 11.15, while another formation consisting of 80 aircraft came in over the Estuary and then turned into Kent attacking towns and aerodromes. Fortunately, very little damage was achieved as RAF fighters intercepted the raiders before they had reached their targets. The RAF lost five aircraft, but lost only two pilots compared to the Germans who suffered seven destroyed, eight probable and thirteen damaged.

The Tide has Turned

The Luftwaffe turned their attentions from the south-east and London to targets in the south-west on the 25th, launching attacks against the Bristol Aircraft Company Works at Filton and other raids against Portland Naval base and Plymouth. The attack against the aircraft works at 11.35 am was considerable with some 90-tons of high explosive being unloaded on the factory by sixty Heinkels of KG55 Gruppen. Sixty workers were killed and another 150 injured.

The production line was seriously affected and it took several weeks to get production running again. RAF fighters of No. 152, 238 and 609 Squadrons intercepted the force of Heinkels and Messerschmitt 110s as they made their return and accounted for four of the bombers and three of their escorts, in return three RAF fighters were written off, two of the pilots killed.

Pilot Officer Keith Ogilvie, a Canadian from Ottawa had been in combat with No. 609 'West Riding' Squadron and had been lucky that day to survive:

> I was giving a Dornier hell and both his engines were streaming glycol, when there was a gigantic 'pow' and a nice hole appeared in my right wing. Immediately I saw a 109 quite close behind and it was evident he didn't want to be my valentine. I shook him off after he sent another hole through my tail, one up my fuselage exploding in my wireless, and one in my port wing, puncturing the tyre. Certainly my closest call yet.
>
> I caught another chap close to the water, but could only get one engine smoking before my ammo gave out. Nearly turned over on landing, but got away with it.

The attacks against aircraft production continued unabated the next day with a large raid of 100 aircraft against the

The Tide has Turned

Supermarine Aircraft Works at Woolston, Southampton. At 4.30 pm, the enemy formation was assembling over the Brittany coast and heading in towards their target. Over the target they dropped seventy tons of bombs on the factory killing 10 and wounding 30 production workers. The damage caused by the bombing brought production at the factory to be indefinitely suspended. Work carried on though by sending various aircraft sections to smaller factory dispersal sites for completion. Once again the bombers and their escort fighters were engaged and combat was undertaken accounting for six German aircraft, our own losses amounted to eight with three pilots lost.

One of the RAF squadrons that engaged was No. 303 Czechoslovakian Squadron led by Squadron Leader Ronald Kellet aged 31. They engaged the Germans at 16,000 feet over Portsmouth claiming several aircraft destroyed or damaged and suffering two Hurricanes damaged and one written off. Before the squadron had gone into the attack, Kellet reported later that he had received an order over his radio using the official call-sign, to abort the mission; however he decided to press home the attack. Was this a German radio deception tuned into RAF radio frequency? Pilot Officer Bohdan Grzeszczak claimed for a Heinkel 111 probably destroyed in his report he filed with his intelligence officer on return to Northolt:

> One Heinkel He111 engaged three miles south-west of Southampton at low altitude and heading out towards the coast trailing smoke from the port engine. I attacked hitting the fuselage and tailplane. Enemy aircraft veered off and dropped to within 1,000 feet of the water. I was then ordered to rejoin my section, so left enemy aircraft losing height with one engine useless and damaged to an estimated category '3'.

The Tide has Turned

On the 27th September, the Germans launched a raid targeted against the Parnell Aircraft Factory near Bristol. As the enemy raiders were picked up by Radar, local squadrons were scrambled. No. 56 Squadron based at Boscombe Down was ordered to get airborne at 11.05 am. They were given instructions to patrol over Middle Wallop, but they missed the enemy formation coming in across the coast. They were then vectored by the controller to fly towards the Isle of Wight at an altitude of 20,000 feet and then turned again towards Bristol to catch the raiders on their return back to France. At approximately 12.00 midday, 'Taffy' Higginson, who was leading Blue Section sighted a formation of twenty Messerschmitt Bf110s on his starboard. He turned his section and went into the attack, picking out one of the enemy aircraft and firing a burst of five seconds. Higginson immediately observed white smoke billowing from the port engine as the 110 dived and climbed in evasive manoeuvres. As Higginson broke away, he was himself attacked by a 109 fighter, who had been ordered to await the return of his comrades near the coastline. Higginson's aircraft was not damaged and he returned to base.

Down in the south-east, four mass raids were the order of the day, firstly at 9.00 am when some 180 aircraft crossed between Folkestone and Dover. 11 Group squadrons were scrambled and met the enemy formations over Maidstone. Forty-five minutes later after being engaged, the German forces retired back across the Channel. The second German incursion came in at 11.47 am, when six formations of 300 bombers and fighters headed towards the Chatham area. Again they were confronted by Spitfires and Hurricanes of 11 Group. Sergeant Ernest Scott of 222 Squadron was flying that day and at 12.40 pm he attacked and destroyed a Messerschmitt 109 over Maidstone. Sadly, later that afternoon Scott was reported as missing in action, so the following report was filled in by the squadron intelligence officer Pilot Officer Raymond. In his report he writes:

The Tide has Turned

This pilot, Sgt Scott, was missing on the patrol following this engagement, without having time to write a report. He stated that at 15,000 feet he encountered a Messerschmitt 109 and carried out a stern attack at 250 yards in one long burst. The enemy aircraft immediately dived and Sgt Scott followed it down and observed it crash in what appeared to be a playground of a school in Maidstone.

Scott remained missing until the 1970s when a crash-site of what was thought to be his aircraft was located at Greenway Court, Hollingbourne, Kent. Unfortunately, the landowner was not agreeable to having his land dug up to recover the aircraft. After many attempts by various groups to try and have the wreckage recovered, Scott's sister Irene and his brother Albert sent a letter to Prince Charles asking for help and support in this matter. Finally the landowner gave his permission. The RAF Salvage and Transportation Flight at Abingdon were sent to undertake the recovery.

When they located the aircraft wreckage they found Sergeant Scott's remains along with some personal belongings and maps. He was finally laid to rest on 1st February 1991, and given a full military funeral at St. John's Cemetery in Margate.

There were other casualties that day including young Philip 'Pip' Cardell of 603 Squadron. His fellow colleague Flying Officer Peter Dexter was flying with 'Pip' that day and remembers the circumstances of Cardell's death.

We were returning to base, when I saw a 109 heading back towards France. I chased him and when within range fired a burst which caused him to throw out white smoke from his starboard wing root. The 109 pulled up to about 500 feet and then he baled out. At this time 'Pip' Cardell was in combat with another 109, which he destroyed. I saw it dive vertically into the sea.

Five more Messerschmitts joined in, diving at us from out of the sun. After a short engagement I saw Cardell break off and head home. While following, I saw he was having difficulties in flying his Spitfire. He then jumped and opened his parachute at five hundred feet. The chute failed to deploy properly and he went into the sea about a quarter of a mile off Folkestone beach.

I circled over Cardell for about ten minutes. No attempt was made whatsoever by the people on the beach to reach him. I then force-landed my aircraft on the beach, commandeered a rowing boat and went out to pick him up. By the time I reached him however, he had drowned.

At day's end, the figures showed a resounding victory for Fighter Command resulting in the biggest loss of Luftwaffe aircraft since the 15th September of 55 aircraft destroyed and many others damaged. British losses were 28 aircraft lost with 20 pilots killed.

Peter Brown who had been serving with No. 611 Squadron up in 12 Group, remembers how more pilots were being sent down to 11 Group to take up the fight. He was himself posted on 28th September:

Towards the end of September, policies were being made at Fighter Command to organize different grades of squadrons with the transfer of operational pilots. No. 611 whom I was serving with at this time had only seen limited action during the battle, was then denuded of pilots who had significant experience as Spitfire pilots, and as a result I was posted south to 41 Squadron.

No. 41 Squadron was based at Hornchurch on the eastern edge of the London Barrage balloon defence. It was a very experienced squadron and had been in action over Dunkirk early in the year. It had already served one tour of operations at Hornchurch in August, returning to its base at Catterick for a rest, before again returning to Hornchurch in September. Casualty reports after the war show that it was the third highest squadron for enemy aircraft shot down, but the second highest squadron in the number of casualties incurred. It was a great squadron, highly professional with very experienced pilots, all with a great sense of humour. I was truly lucky with this posting.

The commanding officer was Squadron Leader Don Finlay who had taken over with little experience in battle. The squadron had lost two previous commanders in earlier fighting; these were Squadron Leader 'Robin' Hood who had been killed and Squadron Leader Robert Lister, who had baled out wounded. The Air Ministry was still thinking in peacetime terms; they were posting squadron leaders to lead us in battle conditions simply by rank and sometimes direct from desk or instructor duties. This was acceptable in times of peace, but fatal against battle-trained Luftwaffe pilots.

The transition from 12 Group to 11 Group was totally traumatic. The speed of events was so fast that for the first two or three trips I saw nothing. Norman Ryder,

my flight commander said 'just stick to me
and you will be alright.'

This I did and soon after he asked me to
fly regularly as his No. 2, which suited me
very well.

The 29th September showed very little activity by the
Luftwaffe except for small nuisance raids against convoys
during the day. Had the Luftwaffe finally conceded the
battle after suffering so many losses on the previous day?

Strangely, the Germans renewed their attacks on the 30th,
perhaps in a one last desperate attempt to regain face for
their leader Hermann Göring, who had promised the
Führer so much; he had said that his beloved Air Force
would wipe the Royal Air Force from the skies. Luftwaffe
squadrons took to the air early morning and began to
formate over the French coast.

The first attack was picked up at 9.00 am consisting of
100 Messerschmitt fighters escorting 30 bombers. A second
wave of enemy aircraft was also observed soon after. Both
formations crossed the English coast at Dungeness and
were met by British fighters. The formations were split by
the Hurricane and Spitfire aircraft diving into them and
none reached further than the outskirts of London before
having to turn back due to ferocity of the defenders.

Another raid developed at 10.50 am, when the all seeing
eyes of the radar defences picked up aircraft approaching
from the Cherbourg area towards the coast of Dorset. The
formation consisted of mainly Messerschmitt Bf110s and
109s, but they were caught by RAF fighters who had been
quickly alerted of the threat and caught the Germans early.
The Messerschmitts turned for home before making
landfall.

During the afternoon more attacks were mounted and the
largest raid that day came in at 3.20 pm, with more than 100
aircraft flying over the Kent and Surrey countryside towards
the capital. The aerodrome at Manston was bombed, but
these exploded on the south-west corner of the field and
caused no damage to either personnel or aircraft.

The Tide has Turned

Pilot Officer Ron Berry was in action that day with 603 Squadron. At 3.30 pm, B Flight was over Redhill when they sighted the enemy formations heading in. Berry reported:

> I was in the guard section with Flight Lieutenant Bolter and sighted a large Balbo of bombers and fighters at various heights below and heading north-west. We were at a height of 30,000 feet. The squadron went into line astern and sailed into the fighters.
>
> I followed Boulter and we attacked a string of six 109s. I caught one up and after a few short bursts the port wing caught fire and it dived down in flames. By the time I was separated from the squadron, several dog-fights could be seen. A few minutes later, I dived out of the sun and gave it a five second burst, closing until I had to break away to avoid collision. The 109 burst into flames and dived and crashed near the Tonbridge area. On landing I learned that Pilot Officer Morton had previously fired at this 109.

The fighting was fierce and unrelenting and many pilots and aircraft were lost. Thirty of the Luftwaffe's aircraft did manage to break through the defences and drop bombs on London. Following this raid, another 180 aircraft were sighted heading in over the areas of Slough and Weybridge covering an area of eight square miles.

Again they were intercepted by Spitfires and Hurricanes from 11 Group. Flight Lieutenant Geoffrey Matheson of 222 Squadron became involved in tackling the enemy fighter escort that provided the bombers with essential cover. At 5.45 pm over Sittingbourne, his squadron went into the attack:

The Tide has Turned

> I was flying No. 2 in the formation which was being led by our CO Squadron Leader Hill. We were flying at 30,000 feet when we sighted an enemy formation of bombers escorted by fighters. We dived to attack the fighters and I picked one out and shot him down in flames. Fighters above us then attacked and I had my tailplane shot, and owing to my engine catching fire, I landed my Spitfire at Sittingbourne Paper Mills. It exploded and was destroyed.

Matheson survived this encounter and was later promoted as a squadron leader in 1941, but was killed on 24th August 1943 while commanding No. 418 Mosquito Squadron at Ford in Sussex.

While the raids over Kent and Surrey had been going on, further south the Germans had launched raids once again against Portland and the Westland Aircraft factory at Yeovil. The first raid had taken place at 10.55 am, when 100 aircraft of Luftflotte 3 comprising of Messerschmitt 109s of JG2 'Richthofen' and JG 53 and Bf110s of ZG 26 'Horst Wessel' crossed over Dorset at St. Alban's Head. They were met by elements of 56 and 609 Squadrons.

Pilot Officer William Higginson of 56 Squadron was flying as Yellow 1 that morning, he reported:

> As Red Section began the attack, I saw glycol pouring from Red 2 and thought that the fighters were coming down to attack us and so I went in to attack them. I climbed up straight to the circling 110s and gave one a three second burst from underneath. The enemy aircraft broke away from the circle and climbed straight up and I followed. A Spitfire attacked the enemy from above and I dived and got in behind him and finished all of my

205

ammunition except 200 rounds. The 110
poured smoke, flames and glycol from
both engines, and dived vertically into
cloud above the sea.

A Messerschmitt was seen to crash by Spitfire Pilot Officer
W.D. Williams of No. 152 Squadron and was later
confirmed as destroyed. It was later discovered that the
aircraft Higginson had attacked had in fact although badly
damaged; succeeded in returning across the Channel and
crash-landed, writing off the aircraft completely. By midday
the Germans had turned for home suffering the loss of
four.

A second raid at 4.35 pm again headed across to Portland,
with two formations of fifty aircraft each heading in, the
first headed to Portland, while the second came in over
Lyme Bay, then turned to join up with the first formation
and penetrated inland for 20-miles. This time the raid
consisted of 43 Heinkel 111 bombers of KG55 escorted by
55 109s of JG2 and JG53 and 40 Messerschmitt 110s of
ZG26. Squadrons in 10 Group were scrambled to meet the
incoming enemy aircraft, these included 56, 87, 152, 213,
238, 504 and 609.

No. 56 Squadron led by Squadron Leader Herbert
Moreton Pinfold climbed to 16,000 feet, coming up sun of
the German formation which was higher at 19,000 feet.
Above the bombers, circling behind was their escort of
Messerschmitt Bf110s. Pinfold ordered his pilots into line
astern and began the attack on bombers from quarter
astern. Pinfold opened the proceedings with a five second
burst on the nearest bomber, but his own aircraft was hit by
enemy gunfire causing glycol to stream out.

Pinfold successfully flew his damaged Hurricane fighter
back to Warmwell and force-landed. He later recalled the
incident:

On the 30th September, we were
scrambled to intercept a heavy formation
of bombers over Portland. The bombers

had fighter support and were heading for an important aircraft factory in Yeovil. In all, I was leading just six Hurricane aircraft for the attack. As squadron leader, I decided not to attack head-on, but to come in from the beam, giving our Hurricanes more of a chance to inflict damage to the bombers with long bursts of machine gunfire.

Within seconds, I was caught up in a frantic dog-fight. I shot down one Dornier, but was hit by return fire. The cooling tank in my Hurricane exploded and my cockpit filled with fumes. I could hardly see a thing, but I managed to nurse my aircraft down safely.

We later discovered the bombing raid had been a disaster. Because of the thick cloud, the Germans had dropped their bombs by mistake on the town of Sherborne, causing huge loss of civilian life. It became known as 'Black Monday.'

Two of the squadrons' Hurricane aircraft had been shot down, but both pilots were safe.

During the fast and furious combats that were raging that day, Sergeant Iain Hutchinson became a victim, when he was shot down, not by a Luftwaffe pilot, but mistakenly by one of our own side:

I was keeping a lookout when I saw a Spitfire behind me, and I turned and banked to give him my plan form, and he shot at me. But this wasn't the first time this had happened to me. Pilot Officer John Broadhurst, a pilot in my own squadron, No. 222, had earlier in the battle shot at me in the distance after one scrap; I can remember seeing his tracer coming over my bow. But thank goodness he missed me.

This other guy however, was quick on the trigger and he hit my petrol tank and tore a six-inch hole in it and it just went up in flames immediately. I then tried to get out as quickly as possible, but I didn't do the right thing in retrospect. If I had had my wits about me, I would probably have slowed the aircraft down and then baled out. But unfortunately I was still travelling at a fair speed.

First of all my parachute became trapped against the canopy hood, because my upper torso was bent back along the fuselage and my legs were still inside the cockpit. Suddenly within an instant, I was travelling free through the air and that was it. I couldn't see very well as my eyes had been burnt. I pulled my ripcord and my parachute opened and I landed rather heavily.

Two old ladies came over to help me; I thought they were from the Women's Defence Force at the time, but it turned out that they were having a picnic lunch and had witnessed me coming down. They had some brandy with them, but they wouldn't let me drink it, they just wet my lips, which didn't do much good.

I don't really remember how long it was before I was picked up; I remember a doctor came and tried to help with my dislocated shoulder, but it was extremely painful. My right trouser leg was pretty well burnt away and I had burn marks up my leg.

I was taken to Uxbridge hospital and there they sprayed the burns with Tannic acid. I understand that I was the last patient to be treated this way. They sprayed all the burns with that; then they developed a crust or scab. This healed alright on my face and arm, but on my leg it went septic, so they had to peel off the scab, which was a painful operation. I was in hospital for about a month, and then rested for a couple of weeks before returning to Hornchurch, where I was given the role of a Duty Pilot.

This last day in September was the last big attempt by day by the German Air Force to launch large bomber raids. The losses had become unacceptable in both men and machines and with the late autumn weather soon approaching, good flying weather would now be at a premium. This had been the 'last throw of the dice' for any chance of invasion.

Records show that between the dates of 10th September through to the beginning of October, the Luftwaffe had lost 463 aircraft against 269 of RAF Fighter Command.

CHAPTER 12
Tactics & Losses

In 1936 Fighter Command was still using many of the aerial tactics and fighter combat manoeuvres and formations which had been developed in the Great War of 1914-18. These had been ideal for that period of biplane dog-fighting at speeds mostly around 120 mph.

With technical advances during this period, fighter aircraft were now exceeding 250 mph. With new Spitfire, Hurricane and Defiant monoplane fighters being developed and the unease on the European continent of the rise of Hitler's Nazi government in Germany, which brought the real possibilities of another war, therefore a new RAF Fighter Command directive in regards to fighter attack tactics was set out and published. These were basically designed to operate against the threat of enemy bomber aircraft, ideal in theory, but no mention at this time was ever suggested that the enemy might be escorted by their own fighter aircraft. The three main planned fighter attacks were as follows:

No. 1 Attack

A succession of single aircraft attacking from astern against a single bomber. Section forms line astern, (stepped down) 800 yards in rear of enemy aircraft. The Section Leader close to optimum range at 400 yards opens and maintains fire at this range, then breaks away downward and returns to flank. The following No.2 and 3 aircraft in turn close to the optimum range and fire when proceeding aircraft breaks away, (attacking from slightly below.)

No.2 Attack

A succession of single fighter aircraft, attacking from astern against a single bomber aircraft. Leading Section forms line astern 800 yards in rear flank of bomber formation. Advance to optimum range at 400 yards (three fighters fan out each behind the target) (If second section, they close on the other flank bomber and close to optimum range and fan out.

No.3 Attack

Two waves of three aircraft in echelon attack. One single seat flight of three aircraft in Vic formation verses three bomber aircraft in Vic formation.

There were of course other forms of attack which were variations on the main three, beam attacks from various angles, quarter attacks etc, and for the very brave head-on.

The German fighter pilots were at an advantage by the start of the war, they had gained much needed experience when they had been used in the Spanish Civil War in 1938. Experimenting with various formations and tactics, they had developed a much manoeuvrable and effect fighting formation labelled the 'finger four', liked to the four outstretched fingers of a hand; unlike the Royal Air Force's rigid Vic formation of three aircraft, where the two pilots on either side of the leading aircraft spent more time concentrating on flying in position to their leader than keeping an eye on what was around in the sky. The German formation of four aircraft was able to fly more openly and scan the sky for the enemy.

When the Battle of Britain began, many casualties suffered by Fighter Command was due mainly to bad tactics or by the complete inexperience of young pilots pushed straight into combat with little knowledge of tactics or what to expect from the opposition.

The following interviews with pilots relate their experience of the tactics being used during the battle and what attacks they preferred personally and also how they related to the loss of fellow comrades during this period. Sergeant Jimmy Corbin, 66 Squadron remembers:

> When you got to a squadron, then you were introduced to so-called tactics, which most of the time were bloody awful. We

were using tight formations, Nothing was discussed on tactics; it was just a case of flying the aircraft, which was bloody stupid. You see, when you are in tight formation, you are in really close, only a few feet apart and therefore it was a full time job to fly in station, keeping in the right place. This meant there was only one chap looking out for you in the air and that was the leader up front. If he got his attack wrong, then we were at the mercy of someone else. Towards the end of the battle, we all started to split up; we learnt this from the Germans, who were using wide formation. If you were 50 yards apart or more, then you'd have twelve people looking out in the sky, not just one. There was always one chap in the squadron who'd got fantastic eyesight. In our case it was a chap, named Owen Hardy, he was a New Zealander and a great friend of mine.

Sergeant John Burgess 222 Squadron

The tactics changed quite a lot; in the initial stages we tended to climb up a lot flying due south from Hornchurch, but this left us always in the inferior position with the Germans always above. The Messerschmitt 109s gathered their height while over France and the Channel, and often came over at least 5,000 feet above us, and of course height is very important in regards to aerial combat. From about the middle of September, we adopted a new tactic which was take-off and head north towards Cambridge and get to about 15 - 16,000 feet and then turn south

212

Tactics and Losses

and from 16,000 feet, then gain more height to cross the Thames at 25 - 30,000 feet. This put us in a much stronger position to meet the 109s at their height. In fact I can remember engagements at that period we quite literally skated over the top of them. You could look down and see them only about 500 feet below us. This gave us the advantage, but the problem was we were always heavily outnumbered and rarely did we enter into an engagement when there would be more Spitfires than 109s. Certainly the days from the end of August until 10th September, the German formations were very large and when you crossed the River Thames you were really in enemy territory. The Germans had the habit of sending over pairs of fighters on hunting sorties, so you had to keep your eyes open all the time.

Pilot Officer Ben Bennions of No.41 Squadron:

The numbers you had to deal with were fantastic, you couldn't believe it, and the sky was black. You would see a batch coming towards you and you would be thinking 'what do we do with this lot. I would try and pick the aircraft off the edges, the tail enders; but sometimes when you met a head-on attack, how we got out the other side unscathed I do not know, but some of our commanding officers adopted this attack and I never saw them again. It was very brave, but I don't think it was the right idea. It took the experienced pilots to work the tactics out. Was it better to approach from beneath? No, because you lose your speed. Is it better to approach from one side? No, because you have full deflection. Is it better to attack from dead astern? No, because you will be in the slipstream. Nobody took time to think about these things, they didn't take time to design the approaches or the tactics. The people on the ground, to them you were just counters on the operations room table.

Pilot Officer Bob Foster 605 Squadron:

There has always been this controversy about the tight Vic formations that we flew in and in hindsight they weren't very manoeuvrable. The problem is when you're flying about the sky in tight formation the only one looking around the sky is the leader; you are concentrating on your formation flying, whereas if you fly in a loose formation then everybody's looking around. We were susceptible to being jumped by 109s, we had weavers at the back, but they didn't always see the enemy coming in or they were themselves shot down and we didn't know they had been shot down. But it was a good tactic, if you were going in against bombers as a squadron. The approach I personally found effective was to attack from a quarter head-on. A head-on attack was very quick and over before you knew it. A beam attack could be dangerous as well as from coming in from the rear. Quite often we would be caught below the bombers by their escorts, but we relied on the Spitfires to take on the 109s.

Tactics and Losses

Pilot Officer Peter Dawburn No. 17 Squadron

> I found that once in combat everything happened so quickly, it's quite difficult to describe really. It's almost instinctive, it was for me anyway and the main thing you had to look out for was that there was nobody getting on to your tail. It was probably different for each pilot. Trying to shoot somebody down was quite difficult, because you had to get right behind them and they would always come at you from different angles. When firing at the aircraft you didn't think about the people inside, you were after the aeroplane.

Sergeant John Burgess:

> I think the spirit of a successful fighter pilot was to look everywhere and never be intimidated by the number of enemy aircraft who were around, because you didn't realise at the time, but they were probably more frightened than you were, because they were miles away from their home territory and deep into enemy territory and if they were caught alone they were finished, either being killed or ending up as prisoners of war. You tried to use your aircraft to the best advantage – you always thought that the Messerschmitt 109 was better than your aircraft, but in performance there was little to choose between them. You always thought that the German pilots were better, but in fact they were virtually the same. The Germans had the advantage

that they had experience, which we didn't have because of their experiences in the Spanish Civil War.

George Bennions:

> I had complete and utter trust in my No.2 and because of that I thought it was a waste of time opening fire at anything more than fifty yards. The most important thing is whether you're firing a hand gun or shotgun or a machine gun, at the point of firing that gun it must be absolutely steady, it must not be swinging from side to side, because if you do, the bullets will fly anywhere. They did not explain this to the pilots that it was essential that at the moment you fired the guns that it should be perfectly stable. Some of the pilots were going in at 300 mph pulling hard on the stick, pressing on the firing button, a complete waste of bullets scattering them all over the sky. I saw chaps blazing away in a stall turn, it was absurd.
>
> I used to prefer going into a quarter attack, turning into almost astern, but not quite, because I didn't want to get caught in the slipstream and then hold the aircraft dead steady and wait for the enemy aircraft to go into the middle of my gun-sight, I would fire off one or two second bursts.

Bob Foster again:

> We were lucky as a squadron unlike others, that we had come down in September with a full compliment and every time we lost people, we instantly got

other replacements in. So we were never down like some squadrons were to six or seven pilots. We had something like eighteen to twenty pilots and twelve aeroplanes. We did manage to have the odd day off and the 15th September was my day off, so I never flew on the big day.

Len Davies of 151 Squadron remembers how he felt about the loss of his comrades:

I was devastated, because there were eleven of us from the auxiliary squadron; we had all done our training together. One of them I remember was Brian Kirk, he went into a Spitfire squadron and another was my close friend Bill Peacock who went to 46 Squadron at Digby, who took over from No. 151 in early September and in matter of days he had been shot down and killed, Kirk was killed that October with 74 Squadron. I think I was one of the few of that eleven that survived. In my own squadron it had been reduced from I think around 26 down to about six, when I was shot down. It was just a bloody shame, but some never had a chance really! If they had had the experience that the German pilots had gained crossing Europe and other places, it might have been a different kettle of fish. You had to be a bit pragmatic about it, if they weren't there the next day, well that was that. It was pretty sad really.

Tactics and Losses

Bob Foster:

Sometimes it sounds a bit heartless, but it was just one of those things you accepted. Some people were far more affected than others and this is not being unkind or anything like that. We lost George Forrester on the second day we were out, we lost 'Jock' Muirhead and Archibald Hope, but there was so much going on that you had to ignore it and carry on.

One chap I shared a room with because we were living out of camp in accommodation at Croydon was a chap named Charles English, he had come down to join us as a replacement; we shared a room together for about a week and then he was killed at the end of September. That was a bit of a shock, he was there and a week later he was gone. The squadron looked after everything; we were not involved with packing up the personal belongings of those that were killed. It was shock, sadness and then get on with the job.

Jimmy Corbin:

Loss of fellow aircrew? It was a hell of a shock, especially if they were really close personal friends, you knew everybody, you weren't necessarily all that friendly, but you got used to it, you couldn't cry after everybody. It was one of those things; you always hoped every time you went up you were going to come back. It was a question of luck, experience and the ability as a pilot. I supposed I had a smattering of all of them. I was made a flight sergeant pilot after about eight months, then a warrant officer pilot, couldn't get any higher than that.

John Burgess:

If I had to analyse my feelings about this period, it would be in three stages. The first would be naivety. On my first sortie I had no fear, though you may think I am boasting, it was like that, I didn't believe I would get shot down and it was all going to be too easy, just waltz up to a German aircraft, open fire and it would explode and that would be the end of that. That naivety only lasted one day and from the second day onwards, I realised that I was in a highly dangerous occupation that I was engaged in. It was a very peculiar feeling; I was only twenty years old at the time.

When you were sitting on the ground, you wanted to go, it was exciting and you were part of a unit and fighting the enemy, and not one person in the squadron ever tried to get out of flying, in fact there was almost a rivalry to be on readiness. I can remember a situation when I jumped into a Spitfire, when we were hurriedly scrambled, which happened to be one of the flight commanders aircraft and I can remember him running towards the aircraft because he was late getting down there, trying to stop me taking off because he wanted to take my place. I taxied out and took off without looking in his direction. That was the sort of spirit you had.

Tactics and Losses

The moment you were told to scramble you got that terrible feeling down in the pit of your stomach and then you'd take off and then you would climb, and when you were climbing you would still have that peculiar feeling, but once action started you were too busy and all you were interested in was avoiding getting killed or trying to shoot down the other aircraft. It was like a dare to some degree, you wanted to see how far you could go without coming to any harm.

You were frightened, but you just wanted to show you could go a bit further than the other man. There was a certain rivalry in this respect. I don't think I ever saw anyone consciously run away, other than when you had too, if a Messerschmitt was behind you, you had to break away otherwise you were dead.

It was not until I was flying sweeps over France the following year that I appreciated what a disadvantage that the Germans were at during the Battle of Britain in fighting over enemy territory. If you got caught and shot at and your engine failed, you were finished, but if you were an English pilot over your own country, if you were shot down or had to do a forced landing, you could fight another day.

On 4th September, Sergeant John Ramshaw aged 24 years was flying with his squadron No 222, when during combat with the enemy he was attacked by Messerschmitt 109 fighters and was shot down. His Spitfire K9962 crashed at Mockbeggar, Collier Street near Yalding in Kent at 1.35 pm. He was dragged from his aircraft severely injured by locals who were quickly on the scene. Sadly he died before reaching hospital. He was buried on 12th September at Queensgate Cemetery with the funeral being attended by many of the local citizens of Beverley, Yorkshire, paying their respects to the young pilot. Over a month later his parents who lived in Beverley, received a letter from Captain James Day the landowner of the farm on which Ramshaw's Spitfire had crashed. He had witnessed the battle in the skies above his farm and the crash. A second letter was to follow giving more details of their son's final moments.

Dear Sir   28th October 1940

 I feel it is my duty to write to you and offer you my sympathy in the loss you have recently sustained by the passing of your son Sergeant Pilot Ramshaw, whose machine crashed on my farm in September. Being one of those who witnessed the accident and an old pilot, I was proud of the way your son stuck to his crippled plane to the last. It may be of some comfort to know more details. If so I shall be happy to tell you more, on hearing from you.
Yours Sincerely
James Day (Captain)

(Second Letter)
Dear Mr & Mrs Ramshaw   7th November 1940

I must admit that at first I hesitated to try and find you, I was so afraid I might cause you even more pain than you already suffered; however I considered it my duty to do so, and so wrote to the Records Officer RAF. You of course are well aware that the aerial fighting over this part of Kent has been almost continuous since the middle of August, especially during September.

 On September 4th at about 1.00 a very big battle was in progress in this district at a great height, when I saw one of our Spitfire machines (which has since proved to be your Son's) loosing height rapidly and it was soon evident that he had trouble with his machine. I then noticed that he had a dead engine and was endeavouring to get out of the fight, but to my disgust, he had been followed down by a Hun, who was attacking him at intervals, when he was flying a machine of which he had no control to fight back. This of course is the opinion I formed when watching the whole time, I have no proof.

The wretched Hun kept it up until within 200 feet of the ground and I am proud to say your son stuck to his machine in spite of all this in an attempt to save it by landing it, when of course I take it he could have jumped when higher up. The country round here is bad for forced landings, being orchards and hop gardens to a large extent. He eventually had to try and get his machine down in one of my Orchards, instead of an adjoining meadow, his judgement having been clouded by the constant attack. It is only natural a crash was unavoidable, and I regret to say it was a complete crash followed by fire. But most fortunate, the two men who arrived first were able to get your son clear of the flames.

I was there almost immediately and we did our best to make him as comfortable as possible, although he was then unconscious, and did not speak again. A doctor and ambulance were soon there and I assisted the doctor and he soon informed me that the injuries were such that there was little to be done, he was carefully placed in the ambulance, I think I am correct when I say that I think he passed away before reaching Maidstone Hospital. I am pleased to say that although the crash was a bad one, his injuries were not so bad, the fatal one being at the back of the head which was sustained in the crash. I am confident that he had no serious wounds from the fighting in spite of the merciless attacks made on him. That he died trying to save his crippled machine. I think I resolved to find you when I undid his equipment and his collar and saw his identity disc. I am (as an old Pilot of the last war) still full of admiration for your son and the way he has retained and added his part to the glorious name the RAF has made, in the defence of our homes and country.

We here have seen the huge formations of bombers flying over to London and intercepted here (sometimes over 100 in number) by our boys who shot them down wholesale until now they dare hardly bring a bomber in daylight. If those bombers had been allowed to come and go as they started, all our towns would have been on the ground by now.

Our pilot's who flew Spitfires and Hurricanes in August and September, are in my humble opinion, the greatest heroes this very dear country of ours have ever known. I only hope that a large majority of other parts of the world will realise it all their lives; for they have saved ours. In this small parish of Marden, there have been at least 20 machines shot down, fortunately, mostly German.

I do so hope that I have not increased your sorrow, but I felt half a   story was not what you wanted. Again, please accept my kindest thoughts in your trouble and you must take comfort in the knowledge that your dear one died bravely in the service of his country and the great service of the air.

Yours sincerely,

James Day

The poignant letter from a witness to John Ramshaw's demise, might have brought some relief; knowing of their son's final moments and sacrifice in the service of his country, but many families of those killed during the battle would have had no such details, instead they would have just got the usual telegram from the war department telling them that their son had been killed or was 'missing in action.'

Aircrew killed and recovered were either buried near where they fell or at the family's wishes returned home for a funeral or cremation. In other cases, the Mother and Father or a representative of the family was asked to attend the funeral and special arrangements would be made, issuing special travel permits.

Of the 2,936 pilots and aircrew of Fighter Command who served during the battle, 544 of them were killed, many more suffered terrible wounds and burns, which would mean medical care for many years to follow. Those who did survive, some would carry the scars of battle mentally for the remainder of their lives. 'Lest we Forget.'

CHAPTER 13

The Final Stages

By the beginning of October, the Luftwaffe High Command had more or less come to the conclusion that any chance of knocking out the Royal Air Force had now gone and that an invasion of south-east England would be out of the question. New tactics were to be employed to bring Britain to her knees. Bombing raids against London during the daylight hours were phased out and would be undertaken at night. Never again would the Luftwaffe send mass raids, which had caused them so many casualties during September.

The new tactics now included fighter-bomber sweeps consisting of Messerschmitt Bf 109s and Messerschmitt Bf 110s. The 109s could carry a single 250 kilogram bomb, the Bf110s could carry six bombs, two 250 kilogram and four 45 kilogram devices. Although the bomb loads were small, the fighters had the advantage of speed and surprise and could fly in low if required, to avoid Radar detection along the coast. The sweeps could be large or small, in formations or as single pairs of aircraft. The fast speed of the fighters would allow them to reach London within 20-minutes from take-off.

The first Luftwaffe raid using this new approach was tried on Tuesday 1st October 1940, when several formations of fifty to one hundred fighter-bombers swept over the Channel during the early morning at 7.00 am until late afternoon. Their targets were Portsmouth, Southampton and London. Strangely the German formations did not come in low, but at high level altitude of 25,000 feet. They were detected by Radar and British fighters were scrambled to intercept.

The RAF fighters were vectored on to the interception expecting to have to cope with standard German bombers as they had previously. Climbing up to meet what they believed to be bombers with fighter protection, they were now confronted with just fighters, which was a completely new experience for some RAF pilots.

Once again the RAF fighters were at a height disadvantage, having not been sent off earlier to gain height in time to meet the approaching Germans. Weather conditions were also not favourable as it was a cloudy day and British fighters had difficulty in finding their foe; who were sometimes hidden in cloud. Combat was met and both sides' sustained casualties, the RAF losses amounted to five aircraft, four Hurricanes and one Spitfire; with three pilots killed, the Germans losing two Bf109s with one pilot killed, the other becoming a prisoner of war and a Bf110 with the loss of both crewmen.

This new threat was now subject to urgent discussion among the Fighter Command leaders, Hugh Dowding and Keith Park of 11 Group. It was decided to allow the squadrons time to get airborne and be adequately positioned to counter the German fighter sweeps, that 'standing patrols' be organised between the various aerodromes in the south-east. Patrol lines at a height of 15,000 feet were set and sections of fighters flying at cruising speed could scan the sky for intruders and relay back information as soon as the enemy was detected. They could then meet the threat in a good position to attack.

Air-Vice Marshal Keith Park's instructions which were issued to his operation controllers and commanders gave an outline to the countermeasures that he envisaged using against the Luftwaffe at this time:

> Because of the lack of height reports and the delays from the RDF and Observer Corps information at Group, and the longer time recently taken by squadrons to take off, pairs and wings of squadrons were meeting the enemy formation above them, before reaching the height ordered by Group.
>
> Tip and run raids across Kent by Bf110s carrying bombs or small formations of

The Final Stages

long-range bombers escorted by fighters, give such short notice that the Group controller is sometimes compelled to detail single fighter squadrons that happen to be in the air to intercept enemy bombers before they attack aircraft factories, sector aerodromes or other vital targets, such as docks, Woolwich etc.

Occasionally, reconnaissance Spitfires or Hurricanes from Hornchurch or Biggin Hill are able to sight and report the height and particulars of enemy formations. Moreover, a special fighter reconnaissance flight is now being formed at Gravesend for the purpose of getting information about approaching enemy raids.

'Whenever time permits, I wish Group controllers to get the 'readiness' squadron in company over sector aerodromes, Spitfires at 25,000 feet and Hurricanes at 20,000 feet, and wait until they report or are in a good position before sending them to patrol lines to intercept raids, having a good track in fairly clear weather.

Flying Officer Peter Brown, then flying with 41 Squadron based at Hornchurch recalls this change in tactics and some of the problems the pilots faced:

By October, the pattern of fighting had changed significantly. The Germans had realised that their bomber attacks on London by day were too costly, the plans for invasion in 1940 had been cancelled and with increasing cloud conditions they effectively ceased by October. The Luftwaffe then changed their offensive attacks to Messerschmitt 109s coming over at 25,000 to 30,000 feet escorting

109s with bombs. The speed of operation of course was much faster and we were then operating at heights, which had not been envisaged before.

It was incredibly cold at 30,000 feet; the temperatures were minus 40 degrees centigrade. We had no heating in the cockpit, no heating for the guns and no heating for the windscreen; everything froze up. Sometimes half of the guns wouldn't fire, sometimes when we dived in to attack the windscreen would freeze up and we would have to break off the attack because we could see nothing forward.

The German fighter sweeps continued to come and varied in scale and penetration. On 11th October, the enemy made up to four sweeps, two over Sussex and Kent and two over the Weymouth area in the south-west. A formation of up to 100 Messerschmitts assembled over the Calais area at 10.00 am and crossed the English coast at Hastings. They targeted and dropped bombs on Canterbury, Ashford, Folkestone and Deal. They were supported an hour later at 11.00 am by another formation, this time they targeted the aerodromes at Biggin Hill and Kenley. By 2.15 pm that afternoon an estimated 100 Luftwaffe fighters were observed near Southend at the mouth of the Thames Estuary and another huge formation over the Tonbridge area at 4 pm. British fighters were hurtled into the fray to meet the incoming raiders and many combats took place. At the end of the day's fighting, the RAF Squadrons had flown 949 sorties, but had lost only nine aircraft, seven Spitfires and two Hurricanes with the loss of four pilots and five wounded; the Luftwaffe suffered eight aircraft destroyed.

Sergeant Jimmy Corbin:

The Final Stages

Half way through October nearing the end of the battle, I was posted south again back to 66 Squadron, who were stationed at Gravesend, which wasn't quite as safe as you can imagine. I remember the first time I was really frightened; there were six of us on patrol and we were jumped by thirty plus 109's that was a bit exciting; a typical dog fight ensued. I sprayed a few, but didn't claim, I was too busy looking after myself.

Peter Brown was in combat on 25th October over Ashford, Kent, when he encountered another Messerschmitt sweep:

We were able to bounce a wing of Messerschmitt 109s. I attacked one and opened fire without great success. He rolled over and dived away. I then climbed up and saw at least eight or nine 109s in formation at a slightly lower height. I dived into attack, opened fire on one of the 109s and saw white glycol streaming from the engine. I gave it another burst before it rolled over and disappeared into cloud. I claimed this as a probable, but later it was confirmed. I chased another one out over the sea, but my ammunition had run out, so I returned home.

On the afternoon of the 29th October, German single-engine fighters flew in low-across the Channel and headed inland to attack targets of opportunity, including RAF airfields. One target which was attacked was the aerodrome at North Weald.

At approximately 4.40 pm, just as No. 249 and 257 Squadrons were taking off a surprise attack was made by a formation of Messerschmitt Bf109s, some carrying single bomb loads. In the attack Sergeant Girdwood of 257

The Final Stages

Squadron was burnt to death as his Hurricane was caught in the explosion of one bomb, causing his aircraft to crash.

The rest of the squadrons managed to get off into the air without further casualties. The 109s had dived and dropped about 44 bombs, about 27 falling on the aerodrome, mostly on the flight path. The guardroom, which had only recently been rebuilt following the previous raids, was practically demolished and a hangar which had also received damage was destroyed. Several dispersal huts were destroyed along with a Miles Magister aircraft. Despite the damage to the landing area, it remained operational. There were six fatal casualties and a dozen injured. Two large bombs fell on open ground near to the officer's mess.

In the combat that followed between the North Weald squadrons and the Messerschmitts that were now heading flat out for home, Flight Lieutenant Blatchford of 257 had his aircraft badly damaged, but he returned unhurt, while Polish Pilot Officer Franciszek Surma of the same squadron in Hurricane P3893 was forced to hit the silk at 1,000 feet, landing somewhat unceremoniously in a tree in a pub garden at Matching, he was otherwise unhurt.

No. 249 fared better however, destroying two 109s, claimed by Flight Lieutenant Barton and Sergeant Maciejowski, three probables claimed by Pilot Officer Millington, and Sergeants Stroud and Davidson and damage to three others.

It was also on this day that Benito Mussolini's Italian Air Force, the Reggia Aeronautica was encountered for the first time. This gesture made by the Italian dictator to Hitler was of token support, as most of the Italian aircraft were totally obsolete compared to the German and British and would be totally outclassed. Their bomber units were Nos 13 and 43 Stormos which flew the Fiat BR20 Cicogna twin-engine bomber and their fighters units comprised of No. 18 Gruppo, using Fiat CR 42 Freccia biplanes, No. 20 Gruppo with G.50 Falco monoplane fighters and 172 Squadrilla operating CZ.1007s reconnaissance bombers. The Italians took off that day, eager to show support of their German comrades who were heading for their target of Portsmouth; the Italians headed for Ramsgate.

Pilot Officer Edward 'Hawkeye' Wells, a New Zealander serving with No. 41 Squadron clearly remembers his encounter with the Italians:

> I recall very clearly my first encounter with Italian aircraft over England. On that day No. 41 Squadron was scrambled, ordered to gain maximum height on a vector towards North Foreland. Unfortunately, my Spitfire was slow to start, so the squadron had to leave without me. Within a minute or so my engine fired and as I was keen to join the squadron and already knew the vector to follow. I set off at full boost hoping to catch them up. But the sky is a very big place and by the time I was over Southend, there was no sign of them.
>
> Shortly after this and still climbing I had to enter cloud. At about 10,000 feet I broke cloud to find myself surrounded or so it seemed, by a very loose and open formation of bi-planes flying just above the cloud ceiling. I could not recognise them, but I assumed them to be a friendly training flight which seemed to have lost its way and strayed into a highly operational area.
>
> Almost at once two or three of them opened fire on me at what seemed extreme range. I found this behaviour to be unacceptable, irritating and even slightly dangerous. I turned on the nearest bi-plane and gave him a good burst of three or four seconds. He immediately disappeared into cloud and was not seen again I repeated this performance with

three more aircraft, by which time I had exhausted my ammunition. Spitfires had only about 15 second's fire time. By this time I decided to give up any hope of rejoining 41 Squadron and I returned to Hornchurch.

Here the intelligence officer, who saw my gun-ports blasted open, was all agog to know what had happened to the rest of the squadron. When I told him I had never made contact with them, but that I had been attacked by a formation of bi-planes, he was astonished as I had been. A quick look at the identification chart hanging in the dispersal hut and I was able to positively identify the aircraft as Italian CR42 fighters. I claimed only a damaged, as I had seen some parts fly off one of the targets before he disappeared into cloud. I now believe that all four CR42s must have fallen into the sea somewhere between Southend and North Foreland. As far as I know, the Italian Air Force never came to England again.

Peter Brown reflects on the air fighting during that month:

As an example of the air activity at the end of October, on 27th, the squadron operated three patrols during the day and again on the 29th, so the battle was still going on. The Germans lost 311 aircraft in October; most of them Messerschmitt 109s and for little purpose. It is worth noting, that I did as many operational sorties in the month of October with 41 Squadron in 11 Group, as I did with 12 Group from July through to September. This I think clarifies so clearly the

difference between the load carried by the
two Groups

As the day fighting drew to a close, the RAF night-fighting
defence squadrons of Beaufighter, Blenheim and Defiant
squadrons continued to take to the air, although their
operations had little effect on the Luftwaffe during this
period.

Eric Barwell of 264 Squadron who had fought during the
day battles until his squadron was retired to night-fighting
because of the high casualties sustained by the Boulton Paul
Defiant aircraft. He remembers:

> We were first sent to Northolt to operate,
> but this aerodrome was completely
> surrounded by barrage balloons, not ideal
> when flying at night. Fortunately the
> people at Fighter Command agreed, so
> they then sent us to Luton. We were still
> controlled from Northolt however. This
> caused other problems, as you could only
> hear Northolt if you were above 2,000
> feet. This meant that when you had low
> cloud, you had no contact and it was very
> difficult to get down. We rigged up a radio
> transmission set at our dispersal hut so
> that we could communicate from the
> ground to the aircraft, although this had
> fairly limited range. You had one man on
> the wireless and another outside the hut
> listening for the aircraft. Once you heard
> the sound of the Defiant, the chap on the
> wireless could give the pilot a bearing to
> come in on.
>
> The Defiant could have been an
> excellent night-fighter, but the main snag
> at that time was that the RDF or Radar
> control was pretty poor. The Blenheim
> and Beaufighters were far better with

The Final Stages

> airborne radar or AI, they had better
> controls and we didn't. It was still sheer
> luck if we found an enemy aircraft in the
> blackness of the night sky.

The Battle of Britain is officially recorded to have ended on 31st October 1940, but the Germans continued their heavy night offensive against Britain and the civilian population and industries. The raids would continue nightly well into 1941.

As November heralded the start of winter, the Luftwaffe curtailed their operations by day and concentrated their attacks on the cities of Britain by night, if weather permitted. The Royal Air Force had prevented any chance of Hitler's ambitions of launching an invasion and to secure his complete hold on Western Europe. As Hitler's thoughts and plans now turned eastwards, towards the possible occupation of Russia, Britain had a few months to replenish and strengthen itself for the battles ahead. With the help of the United States, who remained neutral during this period; supplying much need supplies and raw materials, it might be possible to launch the first offensive strikes against the Nazis.

The Battle of Britain had not won us the war, but it had given Britain a lifeline and time to take stock of what would be needed to defeat Hitler.

The men and women of Fighter Command and the British people had stood up and given their all in order to keep their country free. This indeed was their 'Finest Hour.'

APPENDIX A
Fighter Command Pilots & Aircrew who lost their lives during the Battle of Britain.

1 Squadron
P/O D.O.M. Browne 16.8.40
F/Sgt F.G. Berry 1.9.40
P/O J.A.J. Davey 11.8.40
F/Lt H.B.L. Hillcoat 3.9.40
Sgt M.M. Shanahan 16.8.40
P/O R.H. Shaw 3.9.40
Sgt S. Warren 9.10.40

1 (Canadian) Squadron
F/O R.L. Edwards 26.8.40
F/O R. Smither 15.9.40

3 Squadron
F/O G.F. McAvity 19.10.40

17 Squadron
P/O H.W.A. Britton 6.9.40
F/O D.H.W. Hanson 3.9.40
P/O K. Manger 11.8.40
P/O N.D. Soloman 18.8.40
S/Ldr C.W. Williams 25.8.40

19 Squadron
P/O R.A.C. Aeberhardt 31.8.40
Sub/Lt A.G. Blake 29.10.40
Sgt R.R.G Birch 19 Sqdn 13.7.40
P/O E. Burgoyne 27.9.40
Sgt F. Marek 14.9.40
S/Ldr P.C. Pinkham 5.9.40

23 Squadron
P/O A.A. Atkinson 30.10.40
P/O C.F. Cardnell 8.8.40
Sgt L.R. Karasek 25.9.40
P/O E. Orgias 25.9.40
AC2 R.I. Payne 25.9.40
Sgt H.T. Perry 30.10.40
Sgt C. Stephens 8.8.40
F/O H.J. Woodward 30.10.40

25 Squadron
P/O D.W. Hogg 3.9.40
F/O H.M.S. Lambert 15.9.40

F/O M.J. Milet 15.9.40
Sgt J.B. Thompson 31.7.40
LAC J.P. Wyatt 15.9.40

29 Squadron
Sgt R.J. Gouldstone 25.8.40
AC2 A. Jackson 13.10.40
AC2 N. Jacobson 25.8.40
P/O R.A. Rhodes 25.8.40
Sgt C.J. Richardson 31.7.40
Sgt O.K. Sly 13.10.40
Sgt R.E. Stevens 13.10.40
Sgt E. Waite 11.7.40

32 Squadron
Sub/Lt G.G.R. Bulmer 20.7.40
P/O K.R. Gillman 25.8.40

41 Squadron
F/O J.G. Boyle 28.9.40
P/O H.H. Chalder 10.11.40
F/O D.R. Gamblen 29.7.40
Sgt L.A. Garvey 30.10.40
S/Ldr H.R.L. Hood 5.9.40
P/O G.A. Langley 15.9.40
P/O J.G. Lecky 11.10.40
Sgt P.D. Lloyd 15.10.40
F/O D.H. O'Neil 11.10.40
F/O W.J.M. Scott 8.9.40
F/Lt J.T. Webster 5.9.40

43 Squadron
S/Ldr J.V.C. Badger 30.6.41
Sgt J.A. Buck 19.7.40
P/O K.C. Campbell 29.7.40
P/O J. Cruttenden 8.8.40
P/O R.A. De Mancha 21.7.40
F/O J.F.J. Haworth 20.7.40
P/O A.E.A. van den Hove
d'Ertsenrijck 15.9.40
S/Ldr C.B. Hull 7.9.40
Sgt H.F. Montgomery 14.8.40
Sgt D. Noble 30.8.40
P/O J.R.S. Oelofse 8.8.40

F/Lt R.C. Reynell 7.9.40
Sgt D.R. Stoodley 24.10.40
Sgt L.V. Toogood 27.10.40
P/O C.A. Woods-Scawen 2.9.40

46 Squadron
Sgt S. Andrew 11.9.40
P/O J.C.L.D. Bailey 2.9.40
Sgt H.E. Black 9.11.40
Sub/Lt J.C. Carpenter 9.9.40
P/O A.M. Cooper-Key 24.7.40
P/O J.D. Crossman 30.9.40
Sgt G.H. Edworthy 3.9.40
P/O P.S. Gunning 15.10.40
Sgt G.W. Jeffries 8.9.40
Sgt J.P. Morrison 22.10.40
P/O W.B. Pattullo 26.10.40
Sgt W.A. Peacock 11.9.40
F/O R.P. Plummer 14.9.40
F/Sgt E.E. Williams 15.10.40

54 Squadron
F/O J.L. Allen 24.7.40
Sgt G.R. Collett 22.8.40
P/O A. Finnie 25.7.40
P/O W. Krepski 7.9.40
F/O D.J. Sanders 7.9.40
F/Lt B.H. Way 25.7.40

56 Squadron
Sgt R.D. Baker 11.8.40
F/Sgt C.J. Cooney 29.7.40
Sgt J.R. Cowsill 13.7.40
Sgt J. Hlavac 10.10.40
Sgt M.V. Meeson 20.9.40
Sgt T.R. Tweed 15.9.40
F/Lt P.S. Weaver 31.8.40
Sgt. J.J. Whitfield 13.7.40

64 Squadron
F/O C.J.D. Andreae 15.8.40
Sgt L.A. Dyke 27.9.40
Sgt L.R. Isaac 5.8.40
F/O A.J.O. Jeffrey 25.7.40
P/O P.F. Kennard-Davies 10.8.40
Sub/Lt F.D. Paul 30.7.40
Sgt F.F. Vinyard 6.10.40

65 Squadron
P/O F.S. Gregory 13.8.40
F/O F. Gruszka 18.8.40
Sgt M. Keymer 22.8.40
Sgt D.I. Kirton 8.8.40

Sgt L. Pearson 16.10.40
F/Sgt N.T. Phillips 8.8.40
P/O L.L. Pyman 16.8.40
S/Ldr H.C. Sawyer 2.8.40

66 Squadron
Sgt C.A.H. Ayling 11.10.40
P/O G.H. Corbett 8.10.40
F/Lt K. Gillies 4.10.40
F/O P.J.C. King 5.9.40
P/O H.W. Reilley 17.10.40
Sgt A.D. Smith 4.9.40
P/O J.A.P. Studd 19.8.40
Sgt R.A. Ward 8.10.40

72 Squadron
P/O H.R. Case 12.10.40
Sgt M. Gray 5.9.40
P/O D.F. Holland 20.9.40
P/O E.E. Males 27.9.40
P/O J.R. Mather 27.10.40
F/O O. St John Pigg 2.9.40
P/O N. Sutton 5.10.40
F/O E.J. Wilcox 31.8.40
P/O D.C. Winter 5.9.40

73 Squadron
Sgt J.J. Brimble 14.9.40
F/Lt R.E. Lovett 7.9.40
Sgt A.L. McNay 5.9.40
P/O R.A. Marchand 15.9.40

74 Squadron
Sgt D.H. Ayers 23.9.40
P/O F.W. Buckland 8.10.40
P/O D.G. Cobden 11.8.40
Sgt F.W. Eley 31.7.40
P/O H.R. Gunn 31.7.40
P/O D. Hastings 8.10.40
Sgt T.B. Kirk 22.7.41
F/O A.L. Ricalton 17.10.40
F/O P.C.B. St John 22.10.40
Sgt J.A. Scott 27.10.40
P/O D.N.E. Smith 11.8.40
P/O J.H.R. Young 28.7.40

79 Squadron
Sgt H.A. Bolton 31.8.40
F/O G.C.B. Peters 29.9.40
P/O S. Piatowski 25.10.40
Sgt J. Wright 5.9.40

85 Squadron

P/O J.L. Bickerdike 22.7.40
Sgt G.B. Booth 7.2.41
Sgt J.H.M. Ellis 1.9.40
F/Lt H.R. Hamilton 29.8.40
Sgt L. Jowitt 12.7.40
F/O R.H.A. Lee 18.8.40
F/O P.P. Woods-Scawen 1.9.40

87 Squadron
P/O P.W. Comely 15.8.40
Sgt J.H. Culverwell 25.7.40
F/O R.L. Glyde 13.8.40
P/O D.T. Jay 24.10.40
F/Lt R.V. Jeff 11.8.40
S/Ldr T.G. Lovell-Gregg 15.8.40
Sgt S.R.E. Wakeling 25.8.40

92 Squadron
Sgt L.C. Allton 19.10.40
F/O J.F. Drummond 10.10.40
P/O H.D. Edwards 11.9.40
P/O J.S. Bryson 24.9.40
F/O J.F. Drummond 10.10.40
P/O H.D. Edwards 11.9.40
Sgt P.R. Eyels 20.9.40
Sgt E.T.G. Frith 17.10.40
P/O F.N. Hargreaves 11.9.40
P/O H.P. Hill 20.9.40
St T.G. Oldfield 27.9.40
Sgt K.B. Parker 15.10.40
F/Lt J.A. Paterson 27.9.40
F/O A.J.S. Pattinson 12.10.40
F/Sgt C. Sydney 27.9.40
P/O D.G. Williams 10.10.40

111 Squadron
F/Lt D.C. Bruce 4.9.40
F/Lt S.D.P. Connors 18.8.40
P/O J.H.H. Copeman 11.8.40
Sgt. W.L. Dymond 2.9.40
F/Lt H.M. Ferriss 16.8.40
F/O B.M. Fisher 15.8.40
F/O T.P.K. Higgs 10.7.40
P/O J. Macinski 4.9.40
P/O J.W. McKenzie 11.8.40
Sgt R.B. Sim 11.8.40
P/O R.R. Wilson 11.8.40

141 Squadron
Sgt F.P.J. Atkins 19.7.40
Sgt R. Crombie 19.7.40
Sgt A.G. Curley 19.7.40

85 Squadron
F/Lt I.D.G. Donald 19.7.40
P/O R.A. Howley 19.7.40
P/O J.R. Kemp 19.7.40
P/O R. Kidson 19.7.40
P/O D.M. Slatter 19.7.40
Sgt J.F. Wise 19.7.40

145 Squadron
Sgt E.D. Baker 8.8.40
F/O G.R. Branch 11.8.40
P/O A.C. Hamilton 19.7.40
P/O J.H. Harrison 12.8.40
P/O A.R.I.G. Jottard 27.10.40
F/O Lord R.U.P. Kay-Shuttleworth 8.8.40
Sub/Lt I.H. Kestin 1.8.40
Sgt J. Kwiecinski 12.8.40
F/O A. Ostowicz 11.8.40
F/Lt W. Pankratz 12.8.40
P/O L.A. Sears 8.8.40
Sub/Lt F.A. Smith 8.8.40
Sgt J.V. Wadham 12.10.40
P/O E.C.J. Wakeham 8.8.40

151 Squadron
F/O J.H.L. Allen 12.7.40
P/O R. Ambrose 4.9.40
P/O R.W.G. Beley 12.8.40
Sgt F. Gmur 30.8.40
P/O J.R. Hamar 24.7.40
Sgt R. Holder 26.10.40
P/O J.T. Johnston 15.8.40
S/Ldr E.B. King 30.8.40
P/O J.B. Ramsay 18.8.40
P/O M. Rozwadowski 15.8.40
Sgt D.O. Stanley 27.10.40

152 Squadron
P/O H.J. Akroyd 8.10.40
Sgt J.K. Barker 4.9.40
P/O W. Beaumont 23.9.40
Sgt J. Christie 26.9.40
P/O R.M. Hogg 25.8.40
Sgt K.C. Holland 25.9.40
P/O J.S.B. Jones 11.8.40
P/O F.H. Posener 20.7.40
Sgt L.A.E. Reddington 30.9.40
P/O D.C. Shepley 12.8.40
Sgt E.E. Shepperd 18.10.40
Sgt W.G. Silver 25.9.40
P/O T.S. Wildblood 25.8.40
F/Lt LC. Withall 12.8.40

213 Squadron
P/O H.D. Atkinson 25.8.40
P/O S.H.C. Buchin 15.8.40
W/Cdr J.S. Dewar 12.9.40
P/O R.R. Hutley 29.10.40
P/O J.E.P. Laricheliere 16.8.40
Sub/Lt W.J.M. Moss 27.8.40
Sgt P.P. Norris 13.8.40
P/O J.A.L. Philippart 25.8.40
F/Lt L.H. Schwind 27.9.40
Sgt S.G. Stuckey 12.8.40
F/Lt R.D.G. Wight 11.8.40
Sgt G.N. Wilkes 12.8.40
Sgt A. Wojcicki 11.9.40

219 Squadron
P/O R.V. Baron 12.10.40
Sgt E.C. Gardiner 30.10.40
Sgt C. Goodwin 30.9.40
AC2 J.P. McCaul 30.9.40
Sgt G.E. Shepperd 30.9.40
P/O K.W. Worsdell 30.10.40

222 Squadron
Sgt S. Baxter 14.9.40
P/O J.W. Broadhurst 7.10.40
F/O J.W. Cutts 4.9.40
P/O A.E. Davies 30.10.40
P/O H.P.M. Edridge 30.10.40
Sgt J.I. Johnson 30.8.40
Sgt J.W. Ramshaw 4.9.40
Sgt E. Scott 27.9.40
P/O H.L. Whitbread 20.9.40

229 Squadron
P/O G.L.J. Doutrepont 15.9.40
Sgt J.R. Farrow 8.10.40
F/O M. Ravenhill 30.9.40
F/Lt R.F. Rimmer 27.9.40
F/O G.M. Simpson 26.10.40

234 Squadron
P/O W.H.G. Gordon 6.9.40
P/O G.K. Gout 25.7.40
P/O C.H. Hight 15.8.40
F/Lt P.C. Hughes 7.9.40
S/Ldr J.S. O'Brian 7.9.40

235 Squadron
F/Lt F.W. Flood 11.9.40
P/O A.W.V. Green 11.9.40
Sgt G.E. Keel 9.10.40
P/O J.C. Kirkpatrick 9.10.40

P/O R.L. Patterson 18.7.40
Sgt L.H.M. Reece 18.7.40
Sgt B.R. Sharp 11.9.40
P/O N.B. Shorrocks 11.9.40
P/O R.C. Thomas 9.10.40#
Sgt R.Y. Tucker 18.7.40
Sgt R.D.H. Watts 11.9.40
P/O P.C. Wickings-Smith 11.9.40
P/O D.N. Woodger 24.8.40
Sgt D.L. Wright 24.8.40

236 Squadron
Sgt H. Corcoran 20.7.40
S/Ldr P.E. Drew 1.8.40
Sgt H.D.B. Elsdon 18.7.40
Sgt F.A.P. Head 1.8.40
Sgt E.E. Lockton 20.7.40
P/O B.M. McDonough 1.8.40
Sgt D.D. Mackinnon 18.7.40
F/O B. Nokes-Cooper 1.8.40
P/O R.H. Rigby 18.7.40
F/O C.R.D. Thomas 18.7.40

238 Squadron
Sgt S.E. Bann 28.9.40
P/O F.N. Kawse 11.8.40
Sgt S. Duszynski 11.9.40
Sgt G. Gledhill 11.8.40
P/O D.S. Harrison 28.9.40
Sgt V. Horsky 26.9.40
F/Lt D.P. Hughes 11.9.40
F/Lt J.C. Kennedy 13.7.40
Sgt R. Little 28.9.40
F/O D.C. MacCaw 8.8.40
Sgt H.J. Marsh 13.8.40
Sgt C. Parkinson 21.7.40
Sgt L. Pidd 15.9.40
Sgt F.A. Sibley 1.10.40
F/O M.J. Steborowski 11.8.40
F/Lt D.E. Turner 8.8.40
F/Lt S.C. Walch 11.8.40

242 Squadron
P/O J. Benzie 7.9.40
P/O N.N. Campbell 17.10.40
F/O M.G. Homer 27.9.40
Midshipman P.J. Patterson 20.8.40
P/O K.M. Sclanders 9.9.40

245 Squadron
P/O J.J.I. Beedham 7.10.40
Sgt E.G. Greenwood 21.10.40

248 Squadron

P/O C.J. Arthur 27.8.40
P/O C.C. Bennett 1.10.40
Sgt G.B. Brash 1.10.40
Sgt. G.S. Clarke 1.10.40
Sgt R. Copcutt 20.10.40
Sgt R.C.R. Cox 27.8.40
Sgt M.P. Digby-Worsley 19.8.40
P/O S.R. Gane 20.10.40
Sgt W.J. Garfield 13.9.40
P/O M.D. Green 20.10.40
Sgt A. Kay 13.9.40
Sgt B.W. Mesner 13.9.40
Sgt E.A. Ringwood 27.8.40
Sgt J.H. Round 19.8.40
Sgt N.J. Stocks 20.10.40
Sgt W.H. Want 19.8.40

249 Squadron

Sgt E.A. Bayley 10.10.40
F/O P.R.F. Burton 27.9.40
P/O R.D.S. Fleming 7.9.40
P/O M.A. King 16.8.40
Sgt A.D.W. Main 16.7.40
P/O J.R.B. Meaker 27.9.40
P/O W.H. Millington 30.10.40
F/Lt D.G. Parnall 18.9.40

253 Squadron

Sgt H.H. Allgood 10.10.40
F/Lt W.P. Cambridge 6.9.40
Sgt I.C.C. Clenshaw 10.7.40
P/O J.K.G. Clifton 1.9.40
Sgt J.H. Dickinson 30.8.40
P/O C.D. Francis 30.8.40
Sgt W.G. Higgins 14.9.40
P/O D.N.O. Jenkins 30.8.40
P/O W.M.C. Samolinski 26.9.40
S/Ldr H.M. Starr 31.8.40
F/O A.A.G. Trueman 4.9.40

257 Squadron

F/Lt H.R.A. Beresford 7.9.40
P/O C.R. Bonseigneur 3.9.40
P/O J.A.G. Chomley 12.8.40
F.O B.W.J. D'arcy-Irvine 8.8.40
Sgt R.H.B. Fraser 22.10.40
Sgt A.G. Girdwood 29.10.40
F/Lt N.M. Hall 8.8.40
P/O N.B. Heywood 22.10.40
P/O G.H. Maffett 31.8.40
F/O L.R.G. Mitchell 7.9.40
Sgt K.B. Smith 8.8.40

263 Squadron

P/O A.R. Downer 21.7.40

264 Squadron

F/Lt R.C.V. Ash 28.8.40
Sgt B. Baker 26.8.40
Sgt A. Berry 24.8.40
P/O H.I. Goodall 8.10.40
S/Ldr P.A. Hunter 24.8.40
P/O C.E. Johnson 28.8.40
P/O J.T. Jones 24.8.40
P/O P.L. Kenner 28.8.40
P/O F.H. King 24.8.40
Sgt W.H. Machin 24.8.40
Sgt W. Maxwell 26.8.40
F/O D.K.C. O'Malley 4.9.40
P/O W.A. Ponting 24.9.40
Sgt L.A.W. Rasmussen 4.9.40
F/O L.G. Shaw 24.8.40
Sgt R.C. Turner 28.8.40
P/O D. Whitley 28.8.40
Sgt R.B.M. Young 8.10.40

266 Squadron

P/O D.G. Ashton 12.8.40
P/O N.G. Bowen 16.8.40
P/O F.W. Cale 15.8.40
Sub/Lt H.L. Greenshields 16.8.40
Sgt F.B. Hawley 15.8.40
S/Ldr R.L. Wilkinson 16.8.40
P/O W.S. Williams 21.10.40

302 Polish Squadron

F/O J. Borowski 18.10.40
Sgt S.L. Butterfield 11.8.40
F/O P.E.G. Carter 18.10.40
F/Lt T.P. Chlopik 15.9.40
F/Lt F. Jastrzebski 25.10.40
P/O S. Wapniarek 18.10.40
Sgt J.S. Zaluski 17.10.40
P/O A. Zukowski 18.10.40

303 Polish Squadron

Sgt T. Andruszkow 27.9.40
Sgt M. Brzezowski 15.9.40
P/O J. Bury-Burzymski 24.10.40
F/O A. Cebrzynski 19.9.40
Sgt J. Frantisek 8.10.40
F/O W. Januszewicz 5.10.40
F/O L.W. Paskiewicz 27.9.40
Sgt A. Siudak 6.10.40
Sgt. S. Wojtowicz 11.9.40

310 (Czech) Squadron
F/O J.E. Boulton 9.9.40
Sgt J. Chalupa 16.10.40
P/O E. Fechtner 29.10.40
P/O J. Sterbacek 31.8.40

312 (Czech) Squadron
Sgt O. Hanzlicek 10.10.40

401 (Canadian) Squadron
F/O O.J. Peterson 27.9.40

501 Squadron
P/O H.C. Adams 6.9.40
P/O J.W. Bland 18.8.40
F/O P.A.N. Cox 27.7.40
Sgt F.J.P. Dixon 11.7.40
Sgt E.J. Egan 17.9.40
Sgt S.A. Fenemore 15.10.40
P/O V. Goth 25.10.40
P/O E.M. Gunther 27.9.40
P/O F.C. Harrold 28.9.40
P/O D.A. Hewitt 12.7.40
Sgt O.V. Houghton 6.9.40
F/O K. Lukaszewicz 12.8.40
Sgt G.W. Pearson 6.9.40
F/O A.T. Rose-Price 2.9.40
F/Lt G.E.B. Stoney 18.8.40
P/O E.J.H. Sylvester 20.7.40
P/O P. Zenker 24.8.40

504 Squadron
P/O A.W. Clarke 11.9.40
P/O J.V. Gurteen 15.9.40
F/O J.R. Hardacre 30.9.40
Sgt D.A. Helcke 17.9.40
F/O M. Jebb 19.9.40
F/O K.V. Wendel 7.9.40

600 Squadron
AC2 C.F. Cooper 3.10.40
Sgt J.W. Davies 7.9.40
F/O D.N. Grice 8.8.40
P/O C.A. Hobson 13.10.40
P/O P.R.S. Hurst 23.10.40

600 Squadron Cont'd
Sgt F.J. Keast 8.8.40
Sgt A.F.C. Saunders 7.9.40
AC1 J.B.W. Warren 8.8.40

601 Squadron

P/O P. Chaloner Lindsey 26.7.40
F/Lt C.R. Davis 6.9.40
F/O R.S. Demetriadi 11.8.40
P/O W.G. Dickie 11.8.40
F/O M.D. Doulton 31.8.40
P/O W.M.L. Fiske 17.8.40
F/O J. Gillan 11.8.40
Sgt L.N. Guy 18.8.40
Sgt R.P. Hawkings 18.8.40
Sgt D.E. Hughes 3.10.40
Sgt L.D. May 25.10.40
Sgt F. Mills-Smith 25.10.40
F/Lt W.H. Rhodes-Moorhouse 6.9.40
P/O J.L. Smithers 11.8.40
F/O J. Topolnicki 21.9.40

602 Squadron
F/O W.H. Coverley 7.9.40
Sgt D.W. Elcome 26.10.40
P/O H.W. Moody 7.9.40
Sgt M.H. Sprague 11.9.40
Sgt B.E.P. Whall 7.10.40

603 Squadron
P/O N.J.V. Benson 28.8.40
P/O P.M. Cardell 27.9.40
F/Lt J.L.G. Cunningham 28.8.40
P/O R.B. Dewey 27.10.40
F/O C.W. Goldsmith 27.10.40
P/O P. Howes 18.9.40
P/O D.K. MacDonald 28.8.40
F/Lt H.K. MacDonald 28.9.40
F/O H.K.F. Matthews 7.10.40
F/O A.P. Pease 15.9.40
F/O C.D. Peel 17.7.40
F/Lt FW. Rusher 5.9.40
F/O R. McG Waterston 31.8.40

604 Squadron
LAC A.L. Austin 26.8.40
Sgt J.G.B. Fletcher 25.8.40
Sgt C. Haigh 25.8.40

605 Squadron
F/O P.G. Crofts 28.9.40
P/O C.E. English 7.10.40
P/O G.M. Forrester 9.9.40
P/O W.J. Glowacki 24.9.40
F/O R. Hope 14.10.40
Sgt P.R.C. McIntosh 12.10.40
F/Lt I.J. Muirhead 15.10.40
Sgt R.D. Ritchie 9.8.40

240

607 Squadron
F/Lt C.E. Bowen 1.10.40
Sgt. N. Brumby 1.10.40
F/O I.G. Difford 7.10.40
P/O G.J. Drake 9.9.40
F/Lt W.E. Gore 28.9.40
F/Lt M.M. Irving 28.9.40
Sgt J. Lansdell 17.9.40
P/O J.D. Lehahan 9.9.40
P/O S.B. Parnall 9.9.40

609 Squadron
F/Lt D.H. Barran 7.10.40
P/O J.R. Buchanan 27.7.40
Sgt A.N. Feary 7.10.40
P/O G.N. Gaunt 15.9.40
F/O H. Goodwin 14.8.40
P/O R.F.G. Miller 27.9.40
P/O G.T.M. Mitchell 11.7.40

610 Squadron
F/O C.H. Bacon 30.9.40
P/O K.H. Cox 28.8.40
F/O P.J. Davies-Cooke 27.9.40
Sgt S. Island 12.7.40
P/O P. Litchfield 18.7.40
Sgt E. Manton 28.8.40
Sgt W.J. Neville 11.8.40
S/Ldr A.T. Smith 25.7.40
F/Sgt J.H. Tanner 11.8.40
F/Lt W.H.C. Warner 16.8.40
Sgt P.I. Watson-Parker 13.7.40
P/O F.K. Webster 26.8.40

611 Squadron
Sgt K.C. Pattison 13.10.40
Sgt F.E.R. Shepherd 11.9.40

615 Squadron
F/O P. Collard 14.8.40
Sgt D.W. Halton 15.8.40
P/O J. McGibbon 29.9.40
P/O C.R. Montgomery 14.8.40
P/O M.R. Mudie 15.7.40
Sgt P.K. Walley 18.8.40

616 Squadron
F/O J.S. Bell 30.8.40
F/O G.E. Moberly 26.8.40
Sgt M. Ridley 26.8.40
F/O D.S. Smith 28.9.40
Sgt J.P. Walsh 4.8.40
Sgt T.E. Westmoreland 25.8.40

241

APPENDIX B

Nationalities of Battle of Britain Aircrew

Country	No.
United Kingdom	2,341
Poland	145
New Zealand	127
Canada	112
Czechoslovakia	88
Australia	32
Belgium	28
South Africa	25
France	13
Eire	10
USA	9
Southern Rhodesia	3
Barbados	1
Jamaica	1
Newfoundland	1
Total	2,936

BIBLIOGRAPHY

The following books are recommended by the author as essential background reading for those interested in the Battle of Britain and the RAF campaigns of 1939-45.

Aces High, Christopher Shores & Clive Williams, Grub Street, 1994

Battle of Britain Then & Now MkV, Winston Ramsey, After the Battle, 1980

Fighter Squadrons in the Battle of Britain, Anthony Robinson, Arms & Armour, 1987

Fighter Squadrons of the RAF, John Rawling, MacDonald & Co, 1969

Fighter Command's Sergeant Aces of 1940, Richard C. Smith, Mitor Publications, 2007

Hornchurch Scramble, Richard C. Smith, Grub Street, 2000

Honour Restored, S/Ldr Peter Brown AFC, Spellmount Ltd, 2005

Lights of Freedom, George Allen & Unwin Ltd, 1941

Men of the Battle of Britain, Kenneth Wynn, CCB Associates, 2003

The Air Battle of Dunkirk, Norman Franks, Grub Street, 2000

The Battle of Britain, Richard Townsend Bickers, Prentice Hall Press, 1990

The Narrow Margin, Derek Wood & Derek Dempster, Tri-Service Press Ltd, 1990

Documents, Station and Squadron Operations Books, etc, consulted at the National Archive, Kew, London

No. 19 Squadron	Operations Book	Air 27/252
	Combat Reports	Air 50/10
No. 32 Squadron	Combat Report	Air 50/16
No. 41 Squadron	Operations Book	Air 27/424
	Combat Reports	Air 50/18
No. 54 Squadron	Operations Book	Air 27/511
	Combat Reports	Air 50/21
No. 56 Squadron	Combat Report	Air 50/22

No. 65 Squadron   Operations Book   Air 27/593
No. 74 Squadron   Operations Book   Air 27/640
                    Combat Reports   Air 50/32
No. 92 Squadron   Operations Book   Air 27/743
                    Combat Report   Air 50/40
No. 111 Squadron Combat Report   Air 50/43
                    Operations Book   Air 27/861
No. 222 Squadron Combat Report   Air 50/85
No. 249 Squadron Combat Report   Air 50/96
No. 501 Squadron Combat Report   Air 50/162
No. 504 Squadron Combat Report   Air 50/163
No. 603 Squadron Combat Report   Air 50/167
No. 609 Squadron Combat Report   Air 50/171
No. 615 Squadron Combat Report   Air 50/175

RAF Biggin Hill   Operations Book   Air 28/64
RAF Duxford   Operations Book   Air 28/232
RAF Hawkinge   Operations Book   Air 28/345
RAF Hornchurch   Operations Book   Air 28/384
RAF Kenley   Operations Book   Air 28/419/420
RAF Manston   Operations Book   Air 28/512
RAF North Weald   Operations Book Air 28/603
RAF Tangmere   Operations Book   Air 28/815

Courtesy of the Imperial War Museum, Sound Archive, London.
Ref No. 10093, Air-Vice Marshal Harold Bird-Wilson interview
Ref No. 10218, Air Commodore Peter Brothers interview
Ref No. 10871, Squadron Leader Douglas Grice interview
Ref No. 11103, Wing Commander Geoffrey Page interview
Ref No. 12028, Squadron Leader Charlton Haw interview

Remembering the 'Few'

The past

The National Memorial to the Allied aircrew of the Battle of Britain was created in memory of "the Few", the 3,000 brave young men who fought to defend the free world in the summer of 1940. The money to create the memorial on the White Cliffs above Folkestone, where many of the aerial battles were fought, was raised through public subscription.

The present

The Battle of Britain Memorial Trust is responsible for the memorial, a giant, three-bladed propeller carved into the ground topped by the statue of a lone airman sitting on the propeller boss looking out to sea. The squadron badges of the RAF units involved are carved on the boss, while the names of all 3,000 aircrew are listed on a black granite wall nearby. The site also features full-scale Hawker Hurricane and Supermarine Spitfire replicas.

The future?

It costs the Trust £70,000 a year to maintain the memorial as a tribute to those brave young men of 1940. The Trust is now trying to raise enough money to add a facility that will help educate future generations about the significance of the Battle of Britain to the UK and the world.

Your support is crucial if the Trust is to raise the £500,000 it needs to keep the memory of "the Few" alive in this way for generations to come. You can donate to this most worthwhile of causes by contacting Group Captain Patrick Tootal OBE DL RAF (Ret'd.), Hon Secretary of the Battle of Britain Memorial Trust, c/o PO Box 337, Leybourne, West Malling, Kent ME6 9AA. Alternatively ring 01732 870809 or visit battleofbritainmemorial.org

INDEX

Personnel

Index

Index

Index

Index

Flying Training Schools

RAF Airfields & Sectors

Squadrons

Index